BETTER OFF

Than You Think

GOD'S ASTOUNDING
OPINION OF YOU

RALPH HARRIS

Evangel
Publishing House

Nappanee, Indiana 46550

Requests for information should be addressed to:
Evangel Publishing House
2000 Evangel Way
P.O. Box 189
Nappanee, Indiana 46550
Phone: (800) 253-9315
Internet: www.evangelpublishing.com

Cover Design by Larry Stuart
Edited by Kathy Borsa

ISBN-10: 1-928915-95-7
ISBN-13: 978-1-928915-95-9

Printed in the United States of America

7 8 9 0 1 EP 8 7 6 5 4 3 2 1

My deepest love and thanks to my delightful and blameless wife Sarah and my dear and brilliant daughters Ellen and Emma. Without your encouragement, inspiration, and patience, my life and this book would have all the seasoning of cottage cheese.

". . . In *Better Off Than You Think*, Ralph tackles a critical question that virtually all Christians ask themselves at some point in their walks: 'What does God really think of me?' Ralph points out that the well-intended, but self-deprecating, response many give to this question provides the Enemy with much needed ammunition to attack believers at the very core of their faith. Through an examination of Scripture, key individuals in the Bible, and personal testimony, Ralph argues persuasively for the case that God's opinion of us often exceeds our own opinion of ourselves and that we should be empowered by this understanding to pursue even more fervently—and with more confidence—the things of God. . . ."

Lynn Fortner
Senior Pastor, Culver Community Church
Culver City, California

". . . Ralph's engaging style convinced me anew that God isn't twisting my arm to get me to do things His way. Instead, He invites me to discover how uncomplicated it can be to walk with Him, yielding simply to the Holy Spirit as I take a breath and wait in the glorious moment of the 'intentional pause.' I am changed, and it feels wonderful."

Sue Thompson
Author of *The Prodigal Brother*

Table of Contents

Introduction

Come to me, all you who are weary and bur-
dened, and I will give you rest. Take my yoke
upon you and learn from me, for I am gentle and
humble in heart, and you will find rest for your
souls. For my yoke is easy and my burden is
light. (Matthew 11:28-30)

You're in for the greatest of delights if you are familiar with the above passage but not so familiar with the experience.

The single purpose of this book is that you find Jesus and life in Christ—Christianity—deeply satisfying, beyond anything you've ever known. Many of us long haunted by the above passage know Jesus said it, but our desire to know it in experience has been relatively frustrated.

I believe the current work of God is centered upon the theme found above, with the immediate benefit being a happy bunch of God-enamored Christians—it's what God is doing today. While works for God are important, the work *of* God in His people should so thrill us as to make us crazy about Him and gladly dependent. And that's what life is like when you find Him in you as well as around you. The great joy you find will certainly produce sincere works for God, but that's not God's first goal—it's the result. Works for God are a by-product of grace-filled believers who cannot contain the wonderful, deep urgings and desires of the Spirit living within. This is the inheritance of those purchased by Jesus Christ, and He is determined you should have it.

It begins with knowing what God thinks of you. At a seemingly record pace, God is making new and fantastic sons and daughters, tremendous children of His glory through the new birth in Christ. How thrilling is the church—and how thrilling are you! One moment we're in serious trouble with God, and the next we're spot-on perfect, indwelt by God Himself, residents of heaven already, the people of God's delight. What a change! Yet most days that change makes little difference to us. We've lost, or never known, the wonder of the miracle that began with Jesus, "the firstborn among many brothers" (Romans 8:29).

Why? Because we've been deluded into making a lunatic argument with God not so much about who He is and what He is capable of doing, but about who we are and our role in His plan. While He thinks we're one thing—holy, righteous, blameless, and majestic sons and daughters walking the planet—we think we're something else—something way less. God's opinion of us and our opinion of ourselves don't agree. Based on what He did for us through the death and resurrection of Christ centuries ago, He has been making fabulous new creations, actual brothers and sisters of Jesus, for centuries since. But what do we think? "If I'm a brother of Jesus, as bad as I am, I must be the black sheep of God's family!" And Satan, the chief lunatic, alone enjoys the joke.

With that disagreement as our starting point, it's not hard to imagine why our experience with God falls sadly short of our inheritance. Fortunately, God is fed-up with it! He is happily working to awaken us to what He knows is true concerning us so we may live as we are in Christ—the *astounding* children of God!

So prepare yourself—God is working to impress and convince you of what He has done for you and in you. It's a labor He really enjoys! As He increasingly wins you over to His way of thinking about you, you'll increasingly live as you really are because you'll know who you really are. When your opinion of yourself matches up with God's opinion of you, and when who you are lines up with how you live, the glory of God will be stunningly evident! And you'll be living by faith.

You're going to love what you find through the pages of this book. Its message will transform you and become the most natural and satisfying way for you to live. You've been made for that kind of life, and it's time you had it.

Chapter One

Salieri's Game

So we fix our eyes not on what is seen, but on
what is unseen. For what is seen is temporary,
but what is unseen is eternal.
(2 Corinthians 4:18)

Not long ago my wife and I had a home built for us here in Colorado. Having departed the stuffy congestion of Southern California, the expanse of the Rocky Mountains was wonderfully invigorating. Everything seemed new, which—in our case at least—begged for new plans. Nearly everyone enjoyed our enthusiasm and did what they could to assist the rookies in the Rockies. Our home builders worked diligently, landscaping our front yard with Colorado staples such as river rock, aspens, and meadow-like shrubbery. It seemed like the team of workers had it all done perfectly in fifteen minutes. Unfortunately, the backyard was not part of the deal—they left that for me.

Looking at my lineage, anyone would know why I was ill-equipped to tackle such a task. Generations of males in my family have been virtually clueless around lumber, pipe, and cement. Spend five seconds in my garage and you'll know I'm not one of those guys who has every tool known to mankind perfectly laid out or hung up, while anxiously anticipating a mission to Home Depot over the weekend. The only reason I have any tools at all is because I had to buy them to use immediately—like a hammer.

But because we didn't want our daughters playing in a dirt backyard for the next five years, we carefully constructed a meticulous plan. After months of regular wrestling with dirt, trees, rock, shrubs, and demonic sprinkler lines, I felt I had broken out of the cursed line of ineptitude. A perceptive few confirmed my breakout by saying, "Wow. We didn't think you had it in you. *It actually looks good.*"

Finally, the day came for the crowning deed—the laying of the sod. After we had it in place, we christened it with delicately sprinkled water from our perfectly placed sprinklers and celebrated the flawless completion of our plan. Luxurious and unblemished, the forest green lawn proclaimed our magnificent success.

But there was a problem. Out of our eyesight, our lawn was playing the harlot. In what seemed like no time at all, we became convinced that our pristine fescue had been beckoning every nasty plant seed in our state to lay with it. Ugly offspring soon popped out all over our backyard, revealing what had been happening in the darkness without our knowledge and without our permission. Having planned so carefully and worked so hard, I thought my labor was virtually over—I could just stand back and enjoy the view. But for months on end, what greeted a look out any rear window were weeds, weeds, and more weeds.

We hadn't recognized the terrible effect something unseen and unknown could have on our plans. From those days to these, it's war in our backyard. Only now we know what's going on out of sight and we're fighting a little smarter.

The most important arena is not the one right in front of us— the one we can see—but the one out of sight, the one we cannot see. The real story is not first visible but invisible. Long ago God planned for His story, beginning to end, to unfold visibly over centuries of time. Since you and I first began our life of faith, we've been reading our Bibles and looking to that invisible story more and more—it has our attention. Even if we don't look any different and even if the world around us doesn't look any different, our understanding of it all is *far different*.

We now know that there's a lot going on unseen which fashions our faith and which shapes what we experience. We're learning that, in order to live in the visible, we must put our faith in the invisible. This is how we get to know God and it's also how we get to know ourselves. From the moment the Garden doors were shut to Adam and Eve, man's greatest effort has been to live by faith in what he cannot see.

Our faith will drift rudderless if we don't know what's true and happening in the invisible arena. We'll be left confused and frustrated in the visible because that's where God's story is playing out and we'll be left to pulling mysterious weeds out of our lives all of our days. But if we do discover and believe what God says is true and important in the unseen, life will begin to make sense, life will begin to excel—the life which was promised by our Lord Jesus.

In this book we'll look at what God thinks of Himself, but we'll concern ourselves primarily with what God thinks of you. Why is that important? If God and you disagree about who and what you are, your approach to Him and your approach to all of life will be a tangled mess. It cannot be otherwise. This isn't a book on self-esteem with the goal that, after reading it, you'll feel better about yourself. That's not nearly enough. It is a book about accurate self-estimation based entirely upon what God thinks of you, and without question, you'll feel way better about yourself at the end. For the Christian, self-esteem isn't something you work up and get so you can live well, it's something you receive from God because you are well—now go and live! He loves it and is glorified when we believe Him about ourselves and live accordingly. That's the goal.

Fortunately, the way to it will be surprising and incredibly invigorating because it's a certainty that God thinks you're better than you do, and that you're better off in life than you think. (By the way, He's right!)

God thinks He has made you a fantastic, Spirit-born person, quite a bit like Himself, well-recognized throughout the heavens. ✳ If you could right now take a poll of those in the heavenlies, they would all tell you how much you resemble Him. Of course, you'd have to be wary of those of the Liar Clan; they would lie. But even those on the demonic side of things know the truth ✳ about you. You should too.

You're different. And while you have a residence, an identity (mom, dad, brother, sister, lawyer, salesman, etc.), responsibilities, and more, those earthly things are, at best, nice accessories for you and cannot ever match up to the truth about you. No matter how great and excellent your title, no matter how good your family, no matter how great your lawn looks, any *or the opposite*

3

identity you may have in the visible realm will never match up and never be as good as the identity you have in the invisible realm. It's what makes you different.

For sure it's better than you think and *it's more real than anything else*. More than likely, you'll have to be weaned from focusing upon the various titles and roles this visible world has to offer in order to see the majesty of the invisible and to have it count for something. It might not be easy.

Let me show you what I mean. If I told you that Jesus compared believers to Himself, how would you think we might stack up? It's better than you might believe, and it's fundamentally critical you believe it. Speaking about the people the Father had given to Him, Jesus said: "My prayer is not that you take them out of the world but that you protect them from the evil one. They are not of the world, *even as* I am not of it" (John 17:15-16, italics mine).

According to God we're not of this world to the same extent He is not—we match with Him! Can you believe it? You are not *from* or *of* this world any longer, your natural birth having been overcome by your supernatural birth. One began your life, while the other changed it. One birth was of this world, while the other was of another—you're from the same place God is! That's what He thinks; how about you?

Through your new birth in Christ, God changed you from having the same earth-born nature as those still of this world, and now you're actually of Him, sharing in His very nature. You're now far more like Him at the center of your being than you will ever again be like the people of this world. You are different and He wants everyone and everything to know about the great work He has done with you. He brags on you and you might as well know why.

Not aware of how like Him you have become? It's probably because you've accepted and grown accustomed to what this visible world says about you: who you are, what you are, and how you are. Someone invisible labors night and day so that you will have this mistaken identity.

Satan works to fool believers into believing they are better related to the world they can see than they are to the world they cannot see. In essence, *Satan doesn't want you to believe what God thinks of Himself and what God thinks about you*. He's been at work concerning what Christians believe about themselves for a long, long time, employing brilliant tactics against them.

This scheme is well-portrayed in the terrific 1984 Academy Award-winning film, "Amadeus." Best Actor winner, F. Murray Abraham, plays Antonin Salieri, the court-appointed composer to the King of Austria. A talented composer in his own right, Salieri discovers and quickly begins to resent a rather gifted, spotlight-worthy composer, Wolfgang Amadeus Mozart.

Soon Salieri figures out that God lives in Mozart. That He does is made especially obvious by the fact that while Salieri works endless hours and even years to compose anything of any merit, Mozart dashes off the greatest musical pieces ever known virtually overnight and with ease—"As if he were taking dictation!" Salieri hisses. And it galls him, making him furious with God.

Sitting alone and brooding before a large and impressive crucifix, Salieri pulls down the emblem and sets it into a blazing fire. And you can hear the long-practiced, satanic strategy in his words to Jesus: "From now on we are enemies, you and I. Because you choose for your instrument a lustful, boastful, smutty, infantile boy, and give me for a reward only the ability to recognize the incarnation. Because you are unjust, unfair, unkind, *I will block you. I swear it!* I will hinder and harm your creature on earth as far as I am able. *I will ruin your incarnation!*"

For the remainder of the film, Salieri lives to frustrate the God-indwelt Mozart, robbing him of any recognition or joy of the gift of God within him. He is brutally successful, and finally, Mozart wears out and dies a poor man—alone, unhappy, and unfulfilled. Generations since have marveled at the obvious gift of God in Mozart, celebrating God in their love for his music, but Mozart had that joy and knowledge stolen from him. We know who was in Mozart, but Salieri's game was to make certain Mozart did not.

It was Satan's game then and it remains his game today—don't let people know where the invisible God is. Let them think He is *out there*, but don't let them believe He is *in here*. It's a pretty good game, don't you think?

How long has it been since you've <u>marveled</u> at the fact of "Jesus in me!" or had a <u>genuine bit of delight</u> over Him living in you or a good <u>leap for the joy</u> of it? Has it been a while? Then I think the game is *against you.* I think "Salieri" has been about his business with you, seducing you into siding with his estimation of you ("You're nothing special—*just look at you.*") and perhaps of others as well.

That's the game and if he can, he'll get you to play along.Don't think about whether or not the invisible God lives in people and approach them accordingly, think of them according to what they do and how they're doing at life. Think of people based upon what you can see, not based upon what you cannot see. After all, who can say what people are really like when you can't see them, right? Wrong! If God is in the vessel, then you do know what they're really like. They're sons or daughters of God, and they are not best seen by what is visible but by what is invisible!

Do you see?

If we don't see this, we'll be overwhelmed by the visible and our approach to all of life will be twisted. It cannot be any other way. Dominated by the visible, our attraction to it will become a form of addiction—we'll value it and live for it more than we'll value and live for the invisible. The affects will be disastrous because we'll be living not *as we are,* but *as we think* we are. The truth won't have us—a lie will. And nobody lives well in a lie.

Satan would have you to estimate yourself based not upon the world you're *from,* but upon the world you're *in.* And that will not do.

Writing to the church, the apostle Paul wrote: "I have become its *(the church's)* servant by the commission God gave me to present to you the word of God in its fullness—the mystery that has been kept hidden for ages and generations, but is now disclosed to the saints. To them God has chosen to make known among the Gentiles the glorious riches of this mystery, which is *Christ in you,* the hope of glory. We proclaim him, admonishing and teaching everyone with all wisdom, so that we may present everyone perfect in Christ. To this end I labor, struggling with all his energy, which so powerfully works in me" (Colossians 1:25-29, italics mine).

It would be the pinnacle of understatement to say that for centuries, being "near to God" was not without serious issues.

Following Him meant incredible, tragic, strange, and wondrous things would happen. But God *in* man! Is He serious? Think of it—God's likes and dislikes, God's loves, God's abilities, God Himself within man. Consider how He would stand out from there! It would be obvious.

And that's the plan. Perfect. But it's not easy to walk around in your day thinking, God is in me right now, at this very moment and will not leave me. There may not be much to visibly support that. Nevertheless, facts are facts.

But it wasn't always this way. During God's relationship with man under the old covenant, was anyone ever told to offer himself to God? No. Not once. Why not? No one was ever good enough, no one was ever entirely without blame or sin, and so the intimate presence of God was denied him. A spotless, unblemished, and entirely perfect animal was to be offered in his place. *That was acceptable.*

Is it the same now with the new covenant? *Not at all!* "Therefore, I urge you, brothers, in view of God's mercy, to *offer your bodies* as living sacrifices, holy and pleasing to God—this is your spiritual act of worship" (Romans 12:1, italics mine).

Offering your body is an act of worship because you believe what He says about you, the offering; you've been made "holy and pleasing to God"! Through Christ you've become perfectly acceptable. He didn't make you just a believer, He made you an excellent place in which to live. You're compatible! Probably you don't always feel like He's at home in you or that He's entirely happy about His new digs. Yet faith looks to the invisible—not to the touchy-feely—and you know He's there because He says so.

Further, during the former covenant would anyone have gotten together with a few friends, split a case of nice Egyptian ale, and at around midnight snuck into the Holy of Holies? *No, sir!* Why not? *Because God was in there!* Nobody entered that holy place unless he was the High Priest—and then only once a year. It's not at all difficult to imagine he had been prayed-up for weeks, took plenty of the blood of a spotless lamb with him, and had his family tie a rope securely around his waist. That was a little bit of security in case, confirming their fears, brother Levi didn't make the grade (perfect), and they had to drag out the carcass and claim the body. You didn't mess with the Holy of

Holies because God *Himself* was in that temple.

Has it ever struck you that today God's Holy of Holies, the temple where God lives, is *reading this right now?* ␣Wow

Think for a moment on Paul's words to the sloppy Corinthian Christians: "Don't you know that you yourselves are God's temple and that God's Spirit lives in you? If anyone destroys God's temple, God will destroy him; *for God's temple is sacred, and you are that temple*" (1 Corinthians 3:16-17, italics mine).

Haven't you thought of it? Haven't you ever finished your morning coffee and walking out the door to work thought, Well, here I go, God's sacred mobile home into the day . . . No? You're not dumb–Satan's been at work addicting you to the visible so that you find it difficult to live in the invisible. And faith is frustrated.

He worked on Peter too. Because he had been absent from the God-is-making-all-things-new class, Peter received from the Spirit a nightmare revelation that his assessment of people was a tad bit off. Three times Peter was given a dream filled with nasty-looking, misbehaving creatures, which he assumed were in nature as they looked—*nasty*. Not so.

Correcting Peter's view of people and of Gentiles in particular, the Spirit said to him, "Do not call anything impure that God has made clean" (Acts 10:15). In other words, if God has made something brand new or if God has come to live in a man (1 John 4:13), then regardless of his look, attitude, or behavior, he is *brand new*, and God has made for Himself a holy, earthly dwelling place.

Satan knew and fought against it. He fights still. Tactics? Swap the invisible for the visible. *That'll do it.*

Knowing the tactic, Paul cautions and instructs believers where to look in order to live, "So we fix our eyes not on what is seen, but on what is unseen. For what is seen is temporary, but what is unseen is eternal" (2 Corinthians 4:18).

If according to God we've become brand new creations, entirely new creatures (2 Corinthians 5:17) and no longer of this world, then where is that visible? In the invisible! It's in the unseen eternal, in the never-changing arena that we are known for who we really are! Having been changed into sons of God, a look to the unseen arena will always reveal the truth of who we have become.

That's why Paul urges us to keep our gaze *there,* fixing our hearts and thoughts *there.* In the unseen is where we'll find who we really are at all times, during any experience or condition in the visible temporary that is passing away. We don't "set our hearts on things above" (Colossians 3:1-2) in order to feel better about things below. We do it because that's where we'll find ourselves! We're known *there* but we're fairly unrecognizable *here.* *There* (in the unseen, perfectly real, eternal realm), we're got-it-goin'-on, stand-up-and-shout sons of God. *Here* (in the visible, temporary realm), we don't always look so good.

Where do you suppose Satan would like to galvanize our gaze, *there* or *here?* If he can attract the not-of-this-world sons of God to the things and situations of this passing away stage, *here,* might he then be able to affect their thinking? Might he be able to pull off the scam of the millennium by seducing them into believing they are what they do and feel and they are how they behave and think *here,* more so than what God says they truly are *there?* Do you suppose the devil could disrupt their faith, their belief about God and about themselves in relation to Him, and pointing it away from their native land (the heavenly realm), bend it to earthly things, frustrating Designer and designed? With a nod to Groucho Marx, you bet your life.

And it's not hard to again hear Salieri: "*I will block you. I swear it!* I will hinder and harm your creature on earth as far as I am able. *I will ruin your incarnation!*"

So here's what's happened: By demonic concoction many of us have come to believe that our behavior and thought life reveals more about who and what we are than what the Bible says about who and what we are. Perhaps we're straight theologically (it's tucked away somewhere in our head), but practically and dominantly we're twisted and have the two realms, invisible and visible, entangled. When that happens, we exchange the eternal, always true, and unchanging realm for the seen, temporary realm *as reality,* and then everything gets distorted including our life.

We've affixed our gaze on the wrong place. Scripture tells us the importance of shifting our assessment of people away from how they look or behave, etc., to whether they have had a second birth. Although we are to no longer regard anyone from a worldly point of view (2 Corinthians 5:16), we still fall prey to the temporary temptation. When we see our failures, struggles, and shortcomings, we begin to believe we are truly a mess in need of a lot of changes. What's wrong with that? Soon we'll become fascinated and fixated with ourselves, more so than with God. And that's tragic. Preoccupation with ourselves is on the way in, and the awe of God, who lives within us, is on the way out.

Transfixed by the visible, the practical relevance of the invisible will slip away, and eternal truth will begin to miss the mark of the heart. We'll begin to implore God to work on us, our misplaced faith missing the fact that He already has. And the separating identification of *there* and *here*, of eternal and temporal, is lost. The practicalities of faith are muddled and confused. What Jesus achieved for Himself by the Cross and Resurrection, the joy of making many the very sons of God, is frustrated. *That was Salieri's Game.* And that's the tactic the devil has been using for a long time.

Brennan Manning writes, "The paltriness of our lives is largely due to our fascination with the trinkets and trophies of the unreal world that is passing away . . . When we are not profoundly affected by the treasure in our grasp, apathy and mediocrity are inevitable. If passion is not to degenerate into nostalgia or sentimentality, it must renew itself at its source. The treasure is Jesus Christ. He is the Kingdom within."

What to do? Where to start? Ask the Holy Spirit to expose every lie you might unwittingly believe, any subtle deception concerning what God thinks of you, what you are, and who you are with Him and how that affects your life. He will do it and you'll find it to be one of the most exhilarating exercises you'll ever undertake. It's also the beginning of a whole new kind of love affair, one which changes your life by bringing you out.

And you'll love that.

Chapter Two

The Pursuit of Trivial Nobility

The creation waits in eager expectation for the sons of God to be revealed. (Romans 8:19)

So how does Satan do it? If what's true about God and us is fantastic beyond measure and if all creation longs for the sons and daughters of God to be revealed as they are, majesty unveiled, how does the devil keep us from taking a look? He makes it relatively irrelevant. And he starts early.

Growing up in Southern California during the 60s and 70s, perhaps my greatest challenge was to learn the skills necessary to win over people I thought worthy of my efforts. The sports fields, hallways, and classrooms of my young life were dignified by a desirable class of nobility whose faces and physiques resembled the gods of Greek mythology (or of Hollywood), whose athletic prowess rivaled legend, and whose scholastic achievement assured them the best places in life. Some of us noticed the nobility and longed for it. For those of us who did, a sort of clandestine covetousness crept into our hearts urging us to join the royals through well-employed techniques sure to gain their acceptance.

Some of us used humor and wit in the hope of joining the elite, and as we grew up, some of us sought to impress through the arts, while still others offered to secure alcohol or even drugs for the gods. Whatever the attempt, admission to royalty was the goal. I suspect ancient Rome must have looked somewhat the same.

While the nobles generally remained noble and few entered their ranks without the goods for genuine acceptance and due pomp, many of us noble wanna-bes learned something ruinous: *how to live as pretenders.* Rejection did not mean an end to our pursuit because the desire still plagued us! Although we believed the nobility before us was true nobility, few of us made the effort to resign ourselves to contented serfdom and a life lived in service to royalty. Instead, a twisted way of life formed, which offered some small hope of successful arrival at the town of Aristocracy. Worse yet, a deception took root revealed by the effort: *we believed we were unfit*. We could do no better than act upon that lie.

Following high school, the college campus provided the perfect opportunity for me to start all over again. Embracing the pretender way of life, I *arrived* as a nobleman, no one the wiser. There I could offer my practiced persona and slip into the pageantry of the recognizably regal. What a stage it was, with a much larger audience.

My little world of desire and experience, it seems, was not so unique. Little did I know that most everyone was making the same attempt as mine, scanning the fields of people, harvesting the look and behavior which achieved a notch up the hierarchy, and offering it as their own. Everyone was everyone's audience. Selection to an honor society, acceptance into a high-standing fraternal organization, a good-looking girlfriend on the arm, an excellent internship, or the reward of a desirable position of employment were the marks of burgeoning nobility and the validation of our pursuit amongst the masses.

We all knew the look and we all watched each other's attempts at recognizable superiority, fearing the dreaded label and lot of the mediocre. My work paid off and I made the grade, gaining membership in the necessary organizations and completing the picture with the just-right girlfriend. I looked noble!

Strutting around campus one day, I was approached by a seemingly safe, middle-aged woman who, blocking my way, asked, "Do you know Jesus? Do you *know* Him?"

Strangely enough I had never before been asked that question, though I had grown up attending church fairly regularly. My answer was a sloppy, undignified, "Ugh, um, well, no, *not like that*. I mean, do I *know* Him? No. Not like that."

Looking into my eyes she asked, "Do you want to?"

I responded, "Well, no, not right now." After all, I was gloriously busy and I was finally having a life I wanted.

She left me with a stab to my heart: "One day I think you will. You're not like all of this, and I think one day you will."

I never saw her again. I never forgot her either. At that time I was certain of only a couple of things, one of which was that Jesus was a cosmic kill-joy. You didn't want to get mixed up with Him because your fun factor was sure to drop off—as in falling off a cliff. That lady bothered me, so I was glad to be rid of her, getting back to my increasingly successful life. And that was the other thing, *"Not like all of this?"* I thought, Oh, yes I am. I'm the best of it too. Move aside lady, I'm on my way.

Several years later, with tons of education under my hat and the seeming respect of my peers, I began my launch toward "career." I had the tools. I had the skills. I had the pedigree and the skins on the wall. And to top it all off? *I finally got God.* That's right, I finally accepted Him into my life after being told that not only would He forgive me of my sins, but He would make my life even better than it was. Wow! *Super* nobility!

Frankly, I hadn't been sure about eternity, an intimidating word meaning forever and ever and ever. I believed in Jesus and did some of the things I thought He wanted and didn't do some of the things I thought He didn't want me to do, but still . . . I had fairly well earned my nobility amongst my peers, carefully maintaining it, keeping it close, but what of *His* approval? And the question bouncing around the inside of my head where no one knew about it was, "What do I have to do to impress Him enough?" And the haunting fear, one from my earlier days of pretending, found a new arena—a new nobility to impress and join if only I could.

I accepted the challenge, "accepted" His invitation to become a Christian, and shortly set about to add this new recognizable royalty to my repertoire. In short order, I was carrying the "right" Bible, had a fish sticker on my car, had a proper pendant around my neck, and had begun teaching Bible studies and children's Sunday School.

Now I had everything! I was set. I was sure to succeed and sure to impress, and no matter the arena, I was complete. Business skills? I had my degree. Social acumen? Long practiced, a veteran. Athletic? In just about every sport I could compete;

bring it on. And spirituality? Now I was even attractive there. I could do it all. Just let me prove it. (I spent years in the attempt.)

Here's what happened. I began to experience that high gift of good Christian living, *stress*. In my day-to-day life, it seemed to me that I now held dual citizenship—earthly and heavenly—with standards and requirements for both. On the one hand, earthly nobility had lots of requirements, most of which were coming along quite nicely, thank you very much. As a salesman, there were clients to impress and contracts to secure, competitors to subdue and bosses to schmooze. On the other hand, my Christian link meant there was God to impress, fellow Christians to inspire, a kingdom to advance, and enemies to thwart.

So several times a week, I sowed seed in invisible, spiritual fields, and the rest of the time I learned how to employ "kingdom principles" such that my visible kingdom advanced all the more. Maybe you know the effort: tithe and lucrative contracts will flow like milk and honey; pray for my boss and favor will rain from above; be honest and humble and I'll be a man of integrity, certain to be exalted; watch my mouth, bless and you will be blessed; and work hard—drat, but okay.

But what I noticed and what made me uneasy was that my invisible life and stature (that which I had with God) was increasingly and unfairly estimated and judged by my *visible* life and stature. If I didn't get a particular contract, if a boss didn't notice me in the way I hoped, or if a longed-for relationship with the woman of my dreams failed to materialize, I believed something was wrong with me. Sure, I could chalk it up to God and His sovereignty, but what if I was missing something or doing something wrong which, if fixed, might make things better? Shouldn't I figure it out? Didn't God want me to figure it out? So I set about to discover what was keeping me unfit and undeserving—reading books, attending seminars and praying harder for things to be better. Weren't they supposed to be? Wouldn't they be if I prayed just right and for a long enough time?

Do you ever back into prayer? You know, enter His throne room by apologizing for nearly everything under the sun because you know you're guilty of plenty, and the only way out is by lengthy repentance? (You'd confess global warming if it would help.) I was trying it out as my new angle with God, when one night, during the lamentations part of my prayer, I heard the Spirit say something odd, in direct conflict with my self-deprecating prayer time. As I expressed regret about who knows what, I said something like, "You *know* how I am, Lord . . ." And before I could go on with my theme, into my mind crashed the following:

"I do, but you do not. I find not one fault with you and love you endlessly. I have made you just right—perfect—and I love you. It is well between you and me." "Pardon me! Are you talking to *me*?" What did He know that I did not? You know that word, flabbergasted? I was that. But as it is with God, His words to me came with life and strength, making them gloriously undeniable. He sounded convinced—who was I to argue? Like a teenager who had just read a love letter from the most desirable girl in school, I reveled in His opinion of me and was instantly obsessed with Him. I did nearly everything I could to find out what He thought of me because if He thought it and it was good—even great—then not only was I altogether different than I had supposed, but so was my life, no pretending necessary. And, unlike the charmed school girl, His amazing opinion of me never wavered.

So I devoured the New Testament. I discovered that I had been in a serious disagreement with God, believing I was something very different than what He knew I was. He thought I was something fantastic, and I thought I was something lowly—how could that not cause stress? I disagreed with Him! What I believed about who I was as a Christian was little different than what I believed about who I was in the world. Born something of a misfit, I had to work hard to reverse the assessment and change myself into something royal in both places. What a lot of work!

Because I believed it, I was valiantly attempting to be just right in both places and to live contentedly with dual citizenship. And that is just not possible; one is far better than the other and must win out. The prized nobility of this world, which I had been rigorously pursuing, was exposed as comparatively inconsequential, filthy rags. What I was in His opinion was far better than anything I could ever have become or achieved in this world. The true nobility given me through the new birth in

Christ made every other pursuit of worldly nobility trivial in comparison, even contradictory. It's that good, it's that high, it's that real.

I believe the confused ranks of today's wanna-be nobles are legion, filing past each other day after day, attempting the climb up the visible ladder of success, and filling offices and stadiums, restaurants and schools, and—far worse—churches. Having grown up with the illusion that there was nothing better than the visual nobility offered through a chosen educational and career path, what appeals most is practical, "how-to-make-it-happen" sermons, books, and seminars which often encourage the illusory pursuit. The offer of a visibly better life is a powerful lure, and it often wins out over the discovery of who God has made us in Christ and how then to live. To be sure, we must pursue something, but if our adversary can keep us relatively disinterested in who and what we have become through the new birth, our pursuit of life will keep us making mud bricks in Egypt! There will be no joy in it because we're not fit for it. The other pursuit, the path which marvels at God's grand opinion of us, means genuine awe and delight, revelation from the Spirit, promised new life, and a timely death to a contradictory way of living. If you were the devil, for which one would you vote?

The way forward is to first recognize *something incredible has happened* which in turn has caused *something incredible to happen to you.* You didn't deserve it and you may not know it, but a profound change has taken place. Referring to Jesus, the writer of the book of Hebrews writes: "Then he said, 'Here I am, I have come to do your will.' He sets aside the first [covenant] to establish the second. And by that will, *we have been made holy* through the sacrifice of the body of Jesus Christ once for all. Day after day every priest stands and performs his religious duties; again and again he offers the same sacrifices, which can never take away sins. But when this priest had offered for all time one sacrifice for sins, he sat down at the right hand of God. Since that time he waits for his enemies to be made his footstool, because *by one sacrifice he has made perfect forever those who are being made holy*" (Hebrews 10:9-14, italics mine).

Think of that. The Bible says that God, through the sacrifice of Jesus Christ, has made us holy already and that He has already perfected those of us who are in Christ. Doesn't that seem *preposterous*? Scripture says that in Christ we've already become the righteousness of God (see 2 Corinthians. 5:21), that we've been made flawless and beyond accusation (see Colossians 1:22), sharing in His nature (see 2 Peter 1:4). It seems ridiculous! But it's true. Where? As we saw in Chapter One, it's true there, in the invisible, eternal realm! And for how long will it be true? For how long will we be the holy, perfect, flawless, and beyond-accusation sons of God? For always! The Bible uses all kinds of marvelous words and phrases which describe us as we have already become in Christ, forever establishing how great His gift is to us. It is perhaps the most humbling point of faith to believe what He believes is true about you, and the wonder of it makes you addicted to the One holding the opinion. What a concept.

Yet most days scarcely any of us gets much of a thrill from the fact. Hang out with a few Christian types and drop the biblical truth that they actually are a select bunch of people, a collection of royal, God-birthed ministers, a spotless and holy group belonging to Him (see 1 Peter 2:9-12) and they'll argue with you! I wonder why that might be. We, the bride of Christ, are certainly not dumb. We've been deceived.

Try this: At church next Sunday set up a table and hang out a sign, "Perfect Christian Survey." Pull up a chair, whip out a notepad, and (if your church is big enough) ask a hundred people if they believe they have become perfect with God who loves them madly. Give me your best estimate of the actual percentage responding, "Why, yes, *I do!*"

During more than twenty years of pastoring, I have posed that question in various ways to perhaps thousands of Christians, many of whom did not know I was a pastor (and thus a member of the get-the-right-answer-or-be-shamed Gestapo). My findings? Fewer than five percent.

Think Satan has been successful? I do too. With the lights coming on and the curtain drawing back, the Spirit (not willing that we should live without the knowledge of how well-off we have become with God) is revealing to us the majesty of His grace to us in Christ. Finding out all about it is in no way a trivial pursuit–it's what He wants for you.

17

An important first step in discovering and living with how amazing His opinion of you is requires a rather odd first look: at your death.

Chapter Three

You Stink!

I have been crucified with Christ and I no longer live, but Christ lives in me. The life I live in the body, I live by faith in the Son of God, who loved me and gave himself for me.
(Galatians 2:20)

Kneeling in prayer on a hardwood floor in Monrovia, California, in the early 1980s, I was thanking and praising God for loving me. I'm not sure why that exercise seems to produce still more of the knowledge of His affection but it does.

As I carried on in love, I was temporarily knocked off balance when I heard the Spirit say, "Give me lust." Well, I knew all about that. There had been many days filled with strong longings for what the love of a desirable woman would mean. A good portion of why I'd gone to school was to ogle. What better place? Most all of my friends shared in what had seemed to us a sort of sport. And if you love the sport, you play it every chance you get.

However, because I had become a Christian, I knew my ogling ways were no longer acceptable. Even though I lived in a fraternity house surrounded by sororities, and the game was on all around me, my continued participation in it repulsed me. So I drew away from the game. No dating. No lingering looks. No going to the beach. No coarse joking. No movies with even a glimpse of onscreen affection. I quit *lusting*. But *it* didn't quit me.

I discovered the necessity of relational boundaries and, because of my former expertise at the game of ogling and lust, I drew them boldly and early. I didn't want anything to do with that powerful feeling and enticement.

So, when the Holy Spirit confronted me about lust, I was at first surprised. "What do you mean?" I wondered. "I'm doing pretty well with that. I've got it under control." Still He persisted and I began to fear. I had come to hate what lust did and had committed myself to war against it. Anytime mutual desire reared up in new relationships with women, I made great attempts at keeping it corralled, fearing the beast within.

"Let it up, son. Let me have it."

I very nearly panicked. To let this beastly part of me back onto the field of life meant failure . . . ugly and awful failure. Trembling with the fear of what might happen, I stammered, "Okay" and removed my inner restraint.

Like a balloon inflated too far, too fast, I felt a sudden rush of awful desire swell my chest—only to burst and be gone. *Gone!*

Had you been walking past my little house at that moment, you'd have heard a long shout of joy rivaling the most delirious yell at a sporting event. I was ecstatic! What had happened I didn't know, but I was not the same. What the Spirit said next led me on a successful quest I want to begin to share with you. "It wasn't you."

For weeks after that I reveled in Christ and in a freedom I had never before experienced. I even tested it—going to classic stumbling grounds like local beaches and raucous parties. The ugly beast was gone. I prized knowing Jesus so much that subsequent relationships with women (I eventually married one of them!) took a back seat, a proper seat, to loving and knowing Him. Anytime an improper thought or feeling urged me toward an improper action (I wasn't spared from temptation), I focused upon my Love, and the repulsive suggestion vanished. It couldn't find the familiar foothold in me it once had. (More about this in the next chapter.)

A verse I had known previously, to no effect, became a secure resting place for me, explaining so much of life:

> I have been crucified with Christ and I no longer live, but Christ lives in me. The life I live in the body, I live by faith in the Son of God, who loved me and gave himself for me. (Galatians 2:20)

To illustrate what I found, I want to ask you a question: What will have to happen in order for you to finally be free from the power of sin? If your answer is along the lines of "I'll have to die," then you're doing well. One more question I'd like you to ask yourself: "As a Christian, when did I die?"

Your answer is right now determining much of the direction and experience of your life. I cannot express how important your true answer is for your life. Because my answer was faulty up until that day in Monrovia, so was my living.

God thinks you already died—had a burial and everything. A crowd saw it all. That you may be unaware of it or that it took place long ago does not diminish the fact.

To the beleaguered Christians at Rome, Paul writes:

> Or don't you know that all of us who were baptized into Christ Jesus were baptized into his death? We were therefore buried with him through baptism into death in order that, just as Christ was raised from the dead through the glory of the Father, we too may live a new life. If we have been united with him like this in his death, we will certainly also be united with him in his resurrection. For we know that our old self was crucified with him so that the body of sin might be done away with, that we should no longer be slaves to sin—because anyone who has died has been freed from sin. (Romans 6:3-7)

Every believer has been baptized or immersed into the death of Christ Jesus. Since many of us have seen Mel Gibson's film portrayal of "The Passion," it's not too difficult to envision the scene at Calvary. Imagining ourselves gathered at the cross, we see Jesus pierced for our transgressions, having taken upon Himself the sins of the world as well as our full punishment. Yet, if we're to be immersed into His death, the picture in our minds must change dramatically. Somehow we've got to get where He is; more accurately, we've got to be put *into Him*.

And so, up we go. Lifted by an unseen hand we are moved closer and closer to Him until we can see the mangled and torn body, blood streaming from His many, terrible wounds. Drawing so close we can hear His tortured breathing and without stopping, each of us disappears into Him, immersed into Christ.

Gone.

Think of the crowd. "Where did Ralph go?"

"Umm . . . he went up there" comes the reply, "into Jesus. He went into Him."

"Are you sure?!"

"Yeah. And now Ralph's gone. I don't think he's ever coming back either."

Gone. You too.

When Jesus died, in Him you died too. Believers were put into Him, which means we'll never have to die for our sins because we already have in Christ! Since God thought it a great idea to put us into Christ, we do not need to die in order for us to gain power over sin because, in Christ, we already have!

Certainly, it is difficult to think you have already died, when there is little evidence to support that. But I was convinced of it when kneeling on the hardwood in Monrovia. I had had many years of knowing what I had been—a lustful ogler—but I had not realized that I wasn't anymore! Because I hadn't realized it even after I became a Christian, I kept watch over myself and restrained myself like a vial of nitroglycerin ready to go off at the slightest bump—"Look out! I'm a big, bad bomb!" With all that nervous effort, what chance did I have of discovering that the former me had been removed at the Cross? I believed I was still a bomb more so than I believed I had become a son, with desires and attributes in keeping with that status. I was attempting to live by faith, but what I believed wasn't true!

Unintentionally, we may send the false message that we haven't been included in Christ's death when we implore Christians to *surrender*.

As I listened to a church radio program this morning, the speaker citing Romans 12:1 said, "Surrendering yourself to God is the key to knowing His will for your life, and I'm embarrassed to tell you that there is so much of me not yet surrendered, not yet totally His. I want to one day get to such a point that I am not 75%, not 85%, not 95%, but 100% surrendered to Him! Then I'll be completely His!" The crowd roared an eager "Amen!"

Shaking my head, I muttered, "Ah, nuts." And in my mind came the imagined picture of several hundred listeners holding loaded pistols to their own heads. I imagined they were imploring themselves with encouraging words such as, "See! What have I been telling you? You have to make the choice to surrender, you hard-hearted jerk! Surrender!"

If Jesus were to have walked into that room right at that moment, what do you suppose He would have said? Is that what God would say to His glorious church, crucified with Christ and chosen before the world began? "*Surrender?*" I don't think so.

"Surrender" means *you're not dead*, but you've been beaten by an opponent, the odds are totally against you, you haven't a hope, so you might as well give up. Is that what you think God is saying to you? Are you still so bad that you need to be threatened with the imaginary gun to your head, forced to give up and give in? If your surrender is what He is after, that might imply that either you are more of a dirty scoundrel than you are a holy saint, or that there are two of you, one good and godly, one bad and devilish. In either case it's not true. You are a new you and there's only one of you. (The next chapter is devoted almost entirely to this.)

After such a passion-filled plea to "surrender," how do you suppose it's going to go for those of us who agree that what we need most to please God is to surrender? We may for a time look good and godly, our behavior matching our zealous determination to be fully surrendered. But before long we'll grow tired of our self-imposed vigil, our strength will wane, and sin and failure will break out all over again. And that's depressing—after all we did it for God. Plus, working hard to keep our presumed-bad selves under the gun, we won't know anything of the grace and workings of God. Neither will we know His friendship. Does that describe you?

What we want is not to surrender, but to *believe*. Christians don't live primarily by doing something tough to themselves but by believing God has already done something tremendous! Believing in the change God has made in us will lead us to do a lot of things (like giving away our money when we could just as well purchase something with it, or serving a challenging neighbor when we could easily avoid him, etc.), but we'll do them because we believe it's now our nature to do so. We'll do it by faith in God about ourselves, agreeing with Him! No one will have to harangue us into doing something godly! In every way, acting godly and doing godly things are the most normal things we can do. Doing those things is really living. But if you don't believe you've been changed, you many not embrace your new normal. Instead, you'll need the gun to get you going. "Surrender!"

Nowhere in the New Covenant is the word *surrender* used. And any time the word *submit* is used for believers, it means that "because you believe" and because of "what you believe," get under His leadership, embrace His will as your own, and you'll be where your life is found. It's found in Him—in what He did, in who He is, in where He is, and in where you are—you're in Him. You're not a stubborn, ill-mannered, nasty son of God. You're a rescued and royal son who wants to live by faith in the One who made you so. The life you're looking for doesn't come at the end of a holy gun barrel or by draping a white flag over your presumed-sorry self but through believing the great Gospel about Him. And that's an incredibly humbling thing, which always leads to believing the great Gospel about yourself. If you're going to believe Him about *Him*, you've got to believe Him about *you*.

What I think Jesus would say to that audience goes something like this: "My wonderful brothers and sisters—I am here for you. I can see that you are fearful, and I can see that you so want to please Me. Then believe Me. You are in Me and I am in you, just as I have said. Have I not chosen you? Have I not done everything to secure you with Me? Rest, then. Believe Me about yourselves—your worries about Me are over. There is no part of you unclean—I have seen to it. What are you looking to do to yourselves which I have not done? What do you find insufficient? The Holy Spirit, who lives in you, will happily provide all that you need—He will see to everything. Trust Me, trust what I have done for you, and you will find rest for yourselves. I will see to it."

Oh, and drop the gun. You've already died. Wasn't one death enough?

The nature of a man predisposed to sin, "the old self" got crucified at the Cross. You and I inherited a nasty nature from our distant relative Adam—a nature which was cut off from God and dead to Him. It was, however, alive to the power of sin. While sin is most often thought of as something we do or as something we fail to do, it is also (and more precisely) a power or a pressing force. Some passages in Scripture actually speak of sin as having a personality of its own.

Speaking to Cain, the Lord said, "If you do what is right, will you not be accepted? But if you do not do what is right, *sin is crouching at your door; it desires to have you,* but you must master it" (Genesis 4:7, italics mine).

Concerning sin, the apostle Paul wrote, "Therefore do not let sin reign in your mortal body so that you obey *its evil desires.* Do not offer the parts of your body to sin, as instruments of wickedness, but rather offer yourselves to God, as those who have been brought from death to life; and offer the parts of your body to him as instruments of righteousness" (Romans 6:12-13, italics mine). While we sure feel evil desires, they are no longer *our* evil desires, but *"its* evil desires."

The change God made for you at the Cross makes you now incompatible with sin. That plays a big part in why you feel awful after committing a sin—you're no longer a match! You don't get along with sin! After becoming a Christian, I hated lust, even if I yielded to it; *before* I was a willing participant. What a change!

That former self, dead to God but alive to sin, was killed. And you and I have received a brand new self with the nature of a son of God. This is why a man must be born again—he has a nature problem.

Paul writes:

And you were dead in your trespasses and sins, in which you formerly walked according to the course of this world, according to the prince of the power of the air, of the spirit that is now working in the sons of disobedience. Among them we too all formerly lived in the lusts of our flesh, indulging the desires of the flesh and of the mind, and were by nature children of wrath, even as the rest. But God, being rich in mercy, because of His great love with which He loved us, even when we were dead in our transgressions, made us alive together with Christ (by grace you have been saved), and raised us up with Him, and seated us with Him in the heavenly *places* in Christ Jesus, so that in the ages to come He might show the surpassing riches of His grace in kindness toward us in Christ Jesus. (Ephesians 2:1-7, NAS, italics mine)

While we'll talk more about this in the next chapter, the words *by nature* in verse three mean "by germination," or "by genetic." Our native disposition could only incur God's wrath because all we could do was satisfy the sinful cravings of our flesh, following after it. If by nature I am an ogler, what would you expect? Ogling certainly felt *natural* to me! But not after I received the new birth in Christ. Now it feels natural and delightful to do what pleases Him—we're a match! We're compatible!

All this is no surprise to God, who always intended to give us His genetics. Taking God's dictation, Ezekiel wrote, "I will give you a new heart and put a new spirit in you; I will remove from you your heart of stone and give you a heart of flesh. And I will put my Spirit in you and move you to follow my decrees and be careful to keep my laws" (Ezekiel 36:26-27).

Because this has all taken place for you through Christ, your Father is doing something concerning you that is amazing—unseen and eternal. He knows you've died already and have been raised and seated in the heavenlies in Christ. So He is spreading the evidence of His work everywhere you go, successfully at all times.

In Paul's second letter to the Corinthian church, he writes, "But thanks be to God, who always leads us in triumphal procession in Christ and through us spreads everywhere the fragrance of the knowledge of him. For we are to God the aroma of Christ among *those who are being saved and those who are perishing. To the one* we are the smell of death; *to the other*, the fragrance of life. And who is equal to such a task?" (2 Corinthians 2:14-16, italics mine).

Following the sequence, to those who are being saved we are the fine fragrance of death. To those who are perishing, we are the enchanting scent of life. Have you caught a whiff? When I go amongst fellow Christians (those who have been saved), I'm reminded that they will never have to die for their sins. That issue has been forever settled in Christ. They need not fear. But many of us have been shortchanged on our amazing security in Christ.

Further, I know that we have all the power over sin we will ever need. While Christians may have begun to live by sight and experience ("I sin, so I must not have power over it"), I have terrific news which will assist them to live by faith—that's the way that works best. And the Holy Spirit loves it when we do! I believe knowing Christians had been crucified with Christ kept Paul focused upon who they actually were, which kept his approach to them on track (1 Corinthians 2:2).

Concerning "those who are perishing," God produces from us a captivating fragrance, an other-worldly beckoning to Himself. This invisible drawing effect induces lost and confused people to wonder when around us. That wonder may come out strangely, but it is genuine wonder nonetheless. "You Christians live so peculiarly! Why bother, anyway?" "All you Christians care about is the Bible! *Bible* this, *Bible* that! What's the big deal?" "Don't tell me you go to church! What a waste! I quit that years ago—why haven't you?" Grudging curiosity from the lost and confused will often come at us in distorted ways, but when you consider how tragically twisted everyone is apart from the One who reverses the twist, why expect anything else? The smell of life is enchanting to them no matter how they look when following the scent. With certainty, you may expect to see some strangely inquisitive people hanging about you.

So next time you're gathered together with a number of Christians, pay attention to what you smell. What odor will be emanating to the pleasure of the heavens? The God-glorifying scent of death.

You stink. Isn't that great?

Chapter Four

Who Is I?

Therefore, if anyone is in Christ, he is a new creation; the old has gone, the new has come!
(2 Corinthians 5:17)

You can't depend on your eyes when your imagination is out of focus. Mark Twain

Living in a remote and unpopulated region of Siberia, Andrei Tolstyk was abandoned in a crude home with the family dog by his mother and father before his first birthday. Astonishingly, the boy survived and for the next seven years his only companion was the dog. Discovered by regional authorities, a police spokesman said of him, "When we approached, he was running about on all fours and growling."

Andrei faces years of difficult training in the use of speech (he didn't know a single word), how to use utensils (he used his mouth alone), how to accept and relate to people (he bit virtually everyone who approached him), how to use a bathroom, how and where to sleep, and more. Doctors and psychologists are uncertain as to whether or not Andrei can ever be taught human behavior so he can lead a normal life. Previous attempts with other children raised in similarly traumatic conditions provide little hope. Sadly, the underlying problem few have ever been able to overcome is that of a fundamental belief; Andrei believes he is more dog than human. Even if he adopts the manners and customs of humans, he will do so only to survive and fit in. Until he begins to believe what all those around him know to be true, Andrei is lost.

I believe something similar is true of many in today's Christian community; they don't know who they are, they don't know what they have become, and so they act, all too often, in keeping with the world in which they live. They have become the very best of this world through a new birth in Christ, having become wonderfully well-off sons of God—still, they act lost.

From seminars to sermons, from books to videos, we're incessantly instructing each other on how to live right. Fathers should act kindly and kingly and here's how. Mothers should be compassionate and capable and here's how. Employees should be conscientious and diligent; bosses fair and insightful and here's how. And the reason? Because God wants you to, that's why. That's how you can obey Him and please Him. But that's not really why.

Raised in a pagan world, we've been rescued and made actual sons of God through the Lord Jesus. If now we attempt to act like Him—unaware we've been *made* like Him or if we adopt the manners and customs of Christ in order to "survive and fit in," like Andrei we're still offtrack, even if we have the right look. From fathers and mothers, to brothers and sisters, to bosses and employees, we don't act like we should because we don't know who we are. Further, we don't know who we are not.

Considering the astounding change God has made in us, it's to His glory that we find out about it. It will be helpful to uncover any deceptions which might now be hindering your belief, so let me ask you a question. How often do you think something like the following: "I am such an idiot." "I'll never get anything right." "I always do the worst thing." And my personal favorite, "I'm my own worst enemy."

Most, if not all of us, had these kinds of thoughts before believing in Jesus as well as after believing, with one significant difference: after believing in Jesus, our standards for behavior increased dramatically, as did our corresponding potential for failure.

Think of it. Were your standards of behavior, your expectations of how you should and would treat people and situations, higher *before* receiving Christ or *after*? Do you live up to those standards? If not, what's your problem? Many Christians think one of two things: it might be the devil, but more than likely, it's me—I'm the problem. "*I!*"

So, here's the follow-up question I'd like you to ask yourself: "Who *is* I?" And if you're struggling to come up with a definitive answer at this moment, you're not alone. In fact, you're in good company. See if the way Paul wrestled with this makes sense to you. To the Christians at Rome, Paul wrote:

> For what I am doing, I do not understand; for I am not practicing what I would like to do, but I am doing the very thing I hate. But if I do the very thing I do not want to do, I agree with the Law, confessing that the Law is good. So now, no longer am I the one doing it, but sin which dwells in me. For I know that nothing good dwells in me, that is, in my flesh; for the willing is present in me, but the doing of the good is not. For the good that I want, I do not do, but I practice the very evil that I do not want. But if I am doing the very thing I do not want, I am no longer the one doing it, but sin which dwells in me. I find then the principle that evil is present in me, the one who wants to do good. For I joyfully concur with the law of God in the inner man, but I see a different law in the members of my body, waging war against the law of my mind and making me a prisoner of the law of sin which is in my members. Wretched man that I am! Who will set me free from the body of this death? Thanks be to God through Jesus Christ our Lord! So then, on the one hand I myself with my mind am serving the law of God, but on the other, with my flesh the law of sin. (Romans 7:15-25 NAS)

It's not difficult to hear Paul's anguish, and it's somehow comforting to know we're not alone in this wrestling with self. The first seven words in verse fifteen sum up a lot of my life! Indeed, most of us are rightly intrigued with our behavior . . . especially when it's monstrous.

Several years ago my wife and I took our daughters to Disneyland. As we were thoroughly enjoying our day in the park, we met up with some friends who had children the same ages as ours. They had just been on one of the scariest and most exhilarating rides—*The Matterhorn*—and approached us with lots of whooping and carrying on, inviting us to join them on another go of it. Both of our daughters had heard plenty of screaming coming from terrified people on that ride, having walked past it several times earlier in the day. Ellen, our eldest, cast a wary look at the ride and said, "I don't think so. No." Our three-year-old Emma positively sparkled and said, "Yeah!"

The looks my wife and I exchanged meant that we were searching for our own opinion as well as giving the Holy Spirit a moment to weigh in on the issue. Both of us sensed a sort of "green light" and so off we went.

Meandering through the serpentine line gave me plenty of time to tell Emma what to expect. Darting roller coaster cars caught her eyes, and the shrieks coming from the occupants filled the night air, making her eyes wild with delighted expectation and cautious apprehension. Finally our turn came.

When once we were fastened in with Emma securely nestled in my lap, I began to calmly and confidently narrate our progress. As on most roller coasters, to begin with, we went up and up and up and up into the darkness of the mountain, which meant we were very soon to come *down*. At the instant of our descent, Emma let out a low *"Ehhhhhhhhhhhhhhhhhhhh!"* which she never stopped except to get a breath to start it over again. *"Ehhhhhhhhhhhhhhhhhhhh!"* she said, as we zigged and zagged violently through the black, occasionally whizzing out into the night air, only to whiz back inside. I did the fatherly thing and encouraged her at virtually every moment—"Isn't this great, Emma! We're doing fine, really good!" All she said was, *"Ehhhhhhhhhhhhhhhhhhhh!"*

But though I had ridden this ride many years before, I had forgotten one thing. Halfway through the ride and after rounding a turn, the biggest, baddest, nastiest, overgrown, white gorilla with red, laser beam eyes clawed and roared at us from a ledge just above our path. At once, *"Ehhhhhhhhhhhhhhhhhhhh!"* changed dramatically to a much higher and much louder, *"Aaaaaaaaaaaaaaaaaaay!"* The abominable snowman I had forgotten was suddenly Emma's terrible monster and, while into her ear I poured daddy assurances that it was fake and harmless, it took a few turns before *"Aaaaaaaaaaaaaaaaaaay!"* turned again into a more subdued, *"Ehhhhhhhhhhhhhhhhhhhh!"*

But I had forgotten one more thing—there were two of them! Terror returned and Emma's pitch and volume shot right back up again. It wasn't until we neared the end of the ride that she returned to her more normal state of agitation.

Drawing her limp, octopus-like body from the car and having visions of years of therapy for a traumatized Emma, I heard her ask softly, "What's the monster doing now, Daddy? What's he doing?"

Suddenly hoping the scars wouldn't be all that enduring, I said, "Well, he's not real, you know, but he's probably waving his arms and doing that roar thing as other unsuspecting people whiz by. But remember, he's not real, he's just a machine."

And those two words which made my blood pressure go down, "Okay, Daddy," rang sweetly from my daughter. Ah, success . . . except that she asked, "What's the monster doing now, Daddy?" at least two dozen more times before finally falling asleep on the drive home. No matter my answer (and I had what I thought were some really good ones), she was captivated by the thought of the monster and it wouldn't let her go.

I'm sure most parents teach their children pretty well about monsters, whether imagined or pretended (like Mr. Abominable) or real, as in the case of someone who might harm them. We're understandably concerned with monsters. But I'm not so sure we teach our children about the monster they need to know about far more than any other; *the monster within*. Paul had one and you and I do too. Like all monsters, this one is terrible and dangerous, making us feel and do hideous things.

In our passage from Romans 7, what was Paul's biggest problem? Wasn't it doing? In the seven verses from 15-21, Paul uses the little word, *do* twenty-one times! Concerning our behavior, one might say this is where the rubber meets the road. In all the admonitions concerning the behavior of the believer, this is perhaps the most foundational passage in the New Testament.

We know our behavior, feelings, and thought life aren't what they ought to be. So what's our problem? Regarding growing up in Christ, here's the point: as a Christian, you must believe that *you* are not the problem, but *something in you* is.

Paul wrote in verses seventeen and twenty in Romans 7 that when he sinned, it was no longer him who did it. How can that be? Either he was an arrogant cop-out artist with an amazing flair for denial, or he knew what he was talking about. And it wasn't him who sinned. If we ask *where* Paul's problem lay, we begin to understand what led him toward sin; his problem was in his flesh (Romans 7:18). Nothing good lived there! In fact, sin lived in Paul's flesh. Paul's problem wasn't with himself—after all, Jesus had crucified that former self and made him new (as we saw in Chapter Three). Paul's problem was with what *wasn't* crucified—his flesh.

The flesh is a monster, producing monstrous thoughts and feelings, monstrous attitudes, and monstrous behavior! It will never change. One can never train it up or educate it and expect it to act anything but monstrous. But neither Paul nor you nor I *are the flesh*. We have flesh and at times it *has* us, but we are not the flesh!

For a long time that's what we were but not anymore. Jesus made an historic change.

From that terrible day when Adam and Eve passed through the gates of the paradise that was Eden and began their lives in a comparative wasteland, man has become well acquainted with flesh. Having been born into a dependent, life-giving relationship with God, Adam and Eve were blessed with many of the qualities and characteristics which made up the "image of God" (Genesis 1:26-28). With the life of God as his life, man was to steward the garden surroundings as God would. But when Adam chose to do things differently, independently, he and his wife were banished to a quasi life of independence from God, an existence without real life.

God is life—its very source. Everything He does erupts with life. When Adam and Eve were expelled from the garden, they were separated from life and left to do what they could with what they had left—mortal flesh. Those first steps on the other side of the gate were the initial stumbling of empty mankind. Imagine that first night outside the garden for Adam and Eve, newly separated from God and without life for the first time. *Terrifying* would be an understatement.

The shocking realization of what they lost has echoed throughout history, requiring every relative of Adam and Eve to make something of life *without life*, to make a fallen existence work. But no matter how good a functioning man or woman looks, regardless of what they do for their kids and their community, or how well they plan for their retirement, they are without life—they are dust.

Speaking to Adam and Eve and to all who come after them, God said, "By the sweat of your brow you will eat your food until you return to the ground, since from it you were taken; for dust you are and to dust you will return" (Genesis 3:19).

Quoting the Psalmist, Paul writes of the wretched state of man:

> As it is written: "There is no one righteous, not even one; there is no one who understands, no one who seeks God. All have turned away, they have together become worthless; there is no one who does good, not even one." (Romans 3:10-12)

"Worthless." "Not even one." Ouch. It's not easy to admit, is it? Try posting "You and I Are Worthless" as a bumper sticker on your car (or maybe on your neighbors') and see what happens! With centuries of practice, it is now common for men and women to live by the flesh and call it normal—it's all they know because it's all they have. As we've seen, it makes us prey for a terrible and trivial pursuit. But get alone with someone and they might admit that life isn't at all satisfying and that it's empty and doesn't work. You and I know it's because, having been designed for something more, all they have is *flesh.* They're left to walking "in the futility of their mind, being darkened in their understanding, excluded from the life of God . . ." (Ephesians 4:17-18 NAS). No one can live like that. But many of us try—even Christians.

As it was with Adam and Eve outside the gates of Eden, *the flesh* is that part of us which suggests a course for living which results in life without the life of God. Although God lives inside the Christian, living by the flesh means *life without guts.* It's *gutless* because God isn't in it—there's no divine power involved.

How does it happen? Let's take a look.

Each of us has a soul. The soul is what I like to call our *perceiver-expresser*; it feels and thinks and is aware of what's going on all the time, and it looks for a way of expression. Turn on the television or walk into a room full of people or hear the phone ring, and you'll be instantly alert and aware—your perceiver is doing what it does. Your soul perceives something and you feel fear, you feel happiness, you feel sorrow, you feel calm—any number of things. What follows close behind because of the feeling is the need to do something, to make some type of expression, and you'll think, I'd better do something.

At that point your perceiver-expresser searches for input and your flesh quickly suggests an expressive action—*Here's what to do*—often with thoughts and feelings to match. The flesh is all about action or output. It gives no respect to the presence of the Holy Spirit in you, nor to the fact that you are now a spirit. It runs right by you and speaks to your soul—*Get moving!*

And that's where the danger lurks. If you don't believe that your "insides" are vastly different than before you were born again, your soul will connect with your flesh (Thanks for the suggestion—that'll work.), and the outcome or *deeds of the flesh* will express life without God. Even though He lives in you, He won't be involved. The kingdom of God now in you will be powerless and life will be *gutless*. It will be by the flesh and not by the Spirit.

Adam and Eve most likely never grew accustomed to living by the flesh (life without God's life) and were likely haunted all of their days by the memory of life once connected to God. But centuries later, you and I have never known even the haunting, so the desire for true life must come another way.

It might go something like this: Your perceiver-expresser notices you've gained weight, and the thought which follows is that you're not successful because you're fat. Right on cue, flesh offers condemning thoughts—You knew this would happen, fatso!— If you listen to that for more than a few seconds, *flesh* will suggest a course of action, Well, you'll never change, so go ahead and eat a gallon of ice cream! Might as well have a little pleasure since you won't have it any other way—and if there's any ice cream in the freezer, it's a goner. Or flesh might suggest, Buy some workout clothes, get back in the gym, and GET GOING! You really can't live until you get thin . . . but you can do it if you make it your new crusade.

Following your ice-cream binge, you may feel depression, shame, or even rage, and swear you'll never do it again. Or, as with the second example, you may feel a rush of motivation and buy a new wardrobe. Either way, the flesh is having its way with you because God isn't involved in the expression of your life. He's got nothing to do. To be clear, you're not sinning, but neither are you living as you might.

Fortunately, that won't work for long. Since you've been born again and redesigned by God, you now crave what you've never known—God's life! The Holy Spirit will put up a fuss and alert you—you'll feel conflict or like you're just not getting all that you can out of your Christian walk. And you're not because you're not getting real life. While we'll look intently at this in the next few chapters, the new way of living means that you look to the Spirit in you and *He* produces the life. In this instance, the Holy Spirit is also about output. The Bible calls His output *the fruit of the Spirit* (Galatians 5:22). When He is at work in you, when you listen and follow His leading, the expression of your soul will be godly.

Now while you don't always have to wait for the flesh to exert itself before listening for the Spirit, you probably will to begin with. That's okay because you're just waking up to the desire and need of another way of life—you'll get there! So if, after hearing the offering of the flesh concerning your weight, you instead turn to the Spirit, you might hear: It's alright, you know. We can walk together in this little thing. Let's make it something for us to do together. Your life is with me—remember? And I never measure you by the scale—it's not accurate. But I will satisfy you and we'll be together. Living in this way you may feel genuine peace, love, and assurance. Depression and shame will be gone because the life of God will be working in you; the expression which comes through you will make that apparent. You'll have God's life for your life.

That's how important the soul is. It perceives life (accurately or inaccurately) and then expresses what goes on inside. What your perceiver-expresser feels and thinks is not really the problem, so much as what happens because of it—the expression. If you, a spirit-son of God, choose to follow the suggestion of the flesh, you will express the behavior of the flesh—you'll be a fleshly Christian, at least in that moment. You will have returned to a previous way of living when you were gutless, when God did not yet live in you. If, on the other hand, you choose to live by faith and offer yourself to the Holy Spirit now in you, you will express the activity of the Spirit—you'll be a Spirit-led and Spirit-filled Christian. No longer gutless.

Whatever your soul perceives is no longer the problem area of your life. You don't validate your walk with God if you're having good thoughts and feelings, and you don't invalidate your walk if you're having bad thoughts and feelings. That's not the point! Your starting point is not feelings, but spirit—the Holy Spirit in union with your spirit. Beginning with that truth, your life will be influenced by His life.

And that's life.

Through Christ, you and I have been given God's life with a new way to live. Since Jesus, "the way, the truth and *the life*," made His entrance into us, we're not flesh anymore! Jesus has successfully made us spirit, new creations now filled with God, now filled with *life!* Remember? That's why He came in the first place, to give us life (see John 10:10 and 1 John 5:12).

While we know who and what we were born—pagan-natured flesh bags, we know who and what we were born a *second* time—godly-natured spirits, sons designed for life. What a miracle.

You and I know that while we still have a monster (flesh), and can walk in the manner of a monster (by the flesh), we are not monsters! We have an enemy, but we are not an enemy of God; the enemy is not us. God has a problem, but it is not us. We are not God's problem anymore. If we believe we are the problem, if we believe we are the reason for our stumbling and for our sinning against God and against each other, we are deceived. (And the natural course of deception is that we're off course but don't know it.) We'll usually make war on sin which, in our thinking, usually means we make war on ourselves. For example, if I think I'm bad or I'm the problem, then where do my attention and my efforts go? Right at me . . . or the "me" I think I am. And that forces me into a double life. You too.

Luther Price wrote: "Be what you is, not what you ain't; 'cause if you ain't what you is, you is what you ain't." In other words, if you believe you are something (the flesh) when, in fact, you are not, the life you live will be a false one. You won't live as you really are and have become because you'll believe you're something else; you'll live as you ain't.

This is why we must not implore Christians to *surrender* but rather encourage them to *believe*. While it's true that we carry the flesh, that isn't us. Neither does it surrender to God's commands. Paul wrote that the fleshly mind "is hostile toward God; for it does not subject itself to the law of God, for it is not even able to do so; and those who are in the flesh cannot please God. However, *you are not in the flesh but in the Spirit*, if indeed the Spirit of God dwells in you. But if anyone does not have the Spirit of Christ, he does not belong to Him (Romans 8:7-9 NAS, italics mine). Now that you have been reborn and belong to God, "*you are not in the flesh*"! You're no longer found there! You're "*in the Spirit*"! And you're *of* the Spirit!

This is why (falsely identifying ourselves) whenever we implore ourselves to surrender, we add fuel to the false fight! If we believe that part of us which seems stubborn and reluctant to offer itself to God is us, then we've believed the flesh is us and we'll try to command its surrender. Yikes! No wonder we can never seem to do it. Now, look here, flesh—*I'm serious!* I've had it with you and your terrible rule in my life, so I'm ordering you to cease your efforts immediately. You must no longer produce all that lousy, ugly stuff you've long pumped into my life—*no more of that!* Further, you must submit to daily prayer and Bible reading and *like it!* You hear me? *Surrender!* I mean it!

Twisted in our belief, we will invariably be twisted in our efforts. The way out of the distortion is to live by faith and rightly identify the monster. Paul said that if he sinned, it was not him sinning. Who was it? The monster! The flesh! That which Paul used to be but was no longer, ever since he had been remade and given life.

Here's the promise of God and the direction for your new life:

> But if the Spirit of Him who raised Jesus from the dead dwells in you, He who raised Christ Jesus from the dead will also give *life* to your mortal bodies through His Spirit who dwells in you. So then, brethren, we are under obligation, not to the flesh, to live according to the flesh—

for if you are living according to the flesh, you must die;
but if by the Spirit you are putting to death the deeds of
the body, you will live. For all who are being led by the
Spirit of God, these are sons of God. (Romans 8:11-14
NAS, italics mine)

You're no monster—you're a newly made son! And you have
the Spirit of God, and you have *life*. Because this is so, you may
now happily put to death the ugly and awful deeds of the flesh.
(More about that in Chapter Five.)

When sin is evident in your life, it isn't the evidence that you
are still seriously sinister, nor is it what you truly want to do. Sin
is now a fleshly compulsion through the mental and emotional
faculties of your body to harken back to empty days of long ago
by rejecting dependence upon God in order to do something else.
Empty *stumbling*. Life without guts. Your perceiver-expresser has
gone haywire.

Now, what do we do with this? If I offend you, I'll say
something like, "I'm sorry I did that to you. But I'll know where it
came from. If I don't own the offense and apologize to you, I'm
irresponsible and our relationship will be impaired. After all, the
behavior came through me—I'm responsible. However, if I do not
accurately identify the producer of the behavior, I'll be blaming the
wrong thing, most likely the devil or me, and I'll be boxing the air.

So, when you feel like you want to deceive, where does it
come from? When you feel like you want to get angry (and do!),
where does it come from? When you feel like you want to scream
profanities, where does it come from? When you feel lust, when
you feel like you want to avoid the Spirit's leading, when you
feel like you want to jump into sarcasm in order to avoid the
depths of truth, where does it come from? It doesn't come from
you. However, the monster is very good at masquerading as you,
making you think the flesh is you. What a lie that is!

If we think there was, in fact, no death, no crucifixion with
Christ of the former us on the inside (the predisposed to sin, sons
of wrath *by nature* us), then, believing the lie, we will continually
attempt to correct ourselves, straighten ourselves up, make
something out of ourselves, *do something to change* ourselves. And
we'll think God wants us to as well. The implication? He hasn't

changed us, and we're not sons of His! We may have the title, "son," but we don't have the nature—we don't have the genetics.

As long as we believe the lie that the old, *nasty "I"* still lives, same as before at the center of our being, then the apostle Paul's words will have no meaning and no power—"I have been crucified with Christ and I no longer live . . ." (Galatians 2:20). Believing the lie, tragically, we're set up to work against our new, real, actual son of God selves.

But Peter gives us the incredible truth. "His divine power has given us everything we need for life and godliness through our knowledge of him who called us by his own glory and goodness. Through these he has given us his very great and precious promises, so that through them *you may participate in the divine nature* and escape the corruption in the world caused by evil desires" (2 Peter 1:3-4, italics mine).

That beautiful italicized phrase means that you and I have become actual partakers or sharers of the divine genetic. After your new birth in Christ—that's why your desires changed—what delighted you was different, and what grieved you was unlike what saddened you before. You discovered new desires ("I want to read the Bible!"), new delights ("I enjoy worshiping God!"), and new sorrows ("I so dislike sin!") because you had received a new nature with desires, delights, and sorrows to match. You've been re-germinated! I don't know why we talk to each other as if we don't want to do the will of God now—we do!

The apostle John writes, "Yet to all who received him, to those who believed in his name, he gave the right to become children *of* God—children born not of natural descent, nor of human decision or a husband's will, but born *of* God" (John 1:12-13, italics mine). Those final three words, *"born of God"* mean literally, "out of God were birthed." Christians have been born *of* God, not simply *by* God, and may now take part and involve themselves in Him. We're compatible! We've been given a new nature with the genetic code of God Himself, who has birthed us all over again, *birthed us of Himself.*

More than likely, you'll not always feel that you're living up to your genetic connection, but the facts will never be altered. What the Bible says is true of you *is* true of you, whether you feel it or not!

However, that's precisely where your enemy, the devil, will aim his attack. His method will be to induce you to pay particular attention to your feelings, behavior, and thought life and label those things as more indicative of whom you are than of whom the Bible says you are. If he can get you to believe you are what you feel, do, and think about, then the devil will have you. He will have moved you away from the *truth* about you found in the Gospel. Paul writes,

> Once you were alienated from God and were enemies in your minds because of your evil behavior. But now he has reconciled you by Christ's physical body through death to present you holy in his sight, without blemish and free from accusation—if you continue in your faith, established and firm, *not moved* from the hope held out in the gospel. (Colossians 1:21-23, italics mine)

God did all the reconciling necessary even when we were His enemies, even when we were dead in our transgressions (see also Ephesians 2:4-5). In doing so, He made us entirely new and pure and completely free from flaw. Flawless! How could sons of His be less? And He made us to be free from accusation *as long as we do not move from our great hope in the Gospel!* But if we move away, preferring to take our identity from what we see and feel, what will happen to us? We'll no longer be free from the allegations of the enemy and, instead, we'll get beat up all day long. It will only stop when somehow we're put back into our right mind, believing again what God has done for us and to us in Christ Jesus.

Paul writes, "Therefore, if anyone is in Christ, he is *a new creation*; the old has gone, the new has come!" (2 Corinthians 5:17, italics mine). The two Greek words for *new creation* do not mean that we got an upgrade (more RAM for our inner hard drive) or that our slate was wiped clean for a time. No, we have been made an entirely new, original formation. The moment before our new birth we were one thing (a son of wrath by nature), while the moment following, we became a brand-new, unique son of God by nature. Yet, if we don't know it, we might not look for who we have become, and instead believe we're not all that different . . . we're just supposed to do different things now. But that's not true.

So, if you have been busily trying everything you can to make the old you go, you've been deceived into fighting a war that is not taking place. The old you *did* go. If, because of what you see and feel, you've been trying everything you can to make the new you come, you have also been deceived into fighting a nonexistent battle. The new you *did* come. You have a monster but you are no monster. You're a son.

And *that's* the answer to the question "Who is 'I?'"—I am a son.

Chapter Five

The Demolition Derby Drama

What a wretched man I am! Who will rescue me from this body of death? Thanks be to God — through Jesus Christ our Lord! (Romans 7:24-25)

Okay, I admit it—*I can be dramatic*. I don't understand how people can live seemingly unaffected in their day to day, a little smile here, a little frown there, a bit of excitement now and again, and perhaps a momentary little lapse or two into demonstrated anger. I don't get that. Maybe I just do it bigger . . . me and Texas.

But I know they must feel the same battle going on within them that I do every day. I can feel peaceful and secure one moment, tumultuous and frail the next. I can feel loving and loved, and in about a nano second, a sudden surge into the heat of hatred has me rolling my eyes and gasping for air. You know that battle?

Wow! What a cacophony of confusing thoughts and feelings goes on in me! If I'm truly a vessel of God then I must be a broken-down, leaky, little rowboat, worthy only to putter around the bay! You too? What's wrong with us? Too much television? Too much secular music? Too much politics? (Well, yes, but that's another story . . .) Why is there such a battle within? I try hard to have good thoughts and feelings, but the opposite of what I want and like seems ever to crash into me like a sudden car wreck! Why do I seem to have an everyday demolition derby going on inside of me, banging around on my inner race track? Does it mean I'm not doing very well as a Christian?

On the contrary, it's a really good sign. If you and I will pay attention, allowing the inner conflict to do something for us, we'll see incredible results and miraculous outcomes. Bear with me for a bit.

In most dramas I enjoy there is more than one player, and interaction between the characters is what it's all about. I don't want only resolution in my drama either, but journey, battle, sorrow, and meaning—*and* triumph. Every single day of our life that's what's going on in a drama played out within us.

Notice carefully the players in the following passage from the apostle Paul:

> . . . walk by the Spirit *[player #1]*, and you *[player #2]* will not carry out the desire of the flesh *[player #3]*. For the flesh *[#3]* sets its desire against the Spirit *[#1]*, and the Spirit *[#1]* against the flesh *[#3]*; for these *[#1 and #3]* are in opposition to one another, so that you *[player #2]* may not do the things that you please. But if you *[#2]* are led by the Spirit *[#1]*, you are not under the Law. (Galatians 5:16-18 NASB, italics mine)

So here's the question: In our little drama, who are you? Are you player #1? No one's confused about that, you're not the Holy Spirit. Are you player #3? Negative. You and I have what the Bible calls flesh (something we'll always have and which produces awful thoughts and feelings all by itself), but *we are not* the flesh. You picked player #2, right?

You're not the Spirit and you're not the flesh, you're you. (Hang in there . . .) Here it is—if you're player #2, where are players #1 and #3, and *who* is having the fight? If you answered, "They're in me and *they're* having the fight!" go to the head of the class—you've got it! The two of them, the Spirit and the flesh, are having a no-holds-barred brawl on the course of your inner oval! (See? Car racing really *is* from God!) And each is looking for a devastating angle which wins the race.

From your seat within the arena will you ever be able to resolve their conflict? How about bring out the yellow flag and send them to the pits? Or usher them to the bargaining table? Maybe convince them to give a little for the good of both teams? Or introduce mutually agreed upon equipment modifications and restrictions? No. Not ever. *Never.*

If the high goal has been to reduce or restrict inner conflict, as if that were the primary godly battle, then even while feeling the struggle within, there is much kept from you because you've been engaged in the wrong race.

If you and I believe that the conflict within is *our* conflict, we'll marshal virtually every resource we have and wage war over something we cannot resolve. Though we join the right side and employ proper tactics (prayer, Bible reading, fasting, etc.), and even have seasonal pow-wows and put into play offensives designed to finally provide the triumph for which we've been fighting, that crazy conflict keeps happening anyway. The longer we fight the battle that way, the more evidence there is that we're not actually winning anything, we're not taking any of the enemy's turf, nor plundering his strongholds. And, no matter the latest rallying cry, there are great numbers of people who no longer join in, having lost the desire to battle anymore.

Behind the scenes of the struggle, we wonder why we can't end this turmoil we're having. Why does it seem to flare up at the oddest moments? Why don't the victories last? And that ugly thought often running amuck through our thinking will secure our focus: What's *wrong* with me?

Sleepless nights and tumultuous days teach us all that inner turmoil is *indeed terrible*, and something must be done about it. But having become sons of God, the weapons of our warfare are not at all the same as those of not yet sons; *neither are our goals*. We're not simply human anymore—we mustn't fight like one! The battle is for a prize more valuable than anything of this earth. It belongs to us and is worth a ferocious fight.

History shows that few kings enter battle just to battle. Something else—something valuable—makes the fight worth it. If they had more land, more crops, more slaves, then they could be more and do more and they could have more influence. The evidence of their power and wisdom on display in ever-expanding territory is often the goal they seek. Everyone involved knows it's not about the war; it's about the results. And so they fight. That's what the fight within is all about—*results*.

The problem isn't the skirmish itself; the attack is upon our knowing God *in that very moment*. That's what the battle is about—knowing God! And that's what is worth our every effort!

Having already been secured for eternity in Christ, we battle to know God in the midst of the danger and turmoil, allowing for Him who is within us to be active! What we want is to know Him in the fight, so He can do something about it. We're given over to a battle within "so that the life of Jesus may also be revealed in our body" (2 Corinthians 4:10).

Short of salvation, God's greatest gift to us is that we may know Him who now lives within us. It's not difficult to imagine that nearly every battle we encounter, nearly every strategy taken by the enemy is viciously targeting that gift . . . and the result of the gift! And that's why we fight. (More about that in the next chapter.)

Himself no stranger to the battle within, Paul wrote to the Corinthians, "For though we walk in the flesh, we do not war according to the flesh, for the weapons of our warfare are not of the flesh, but divinely powerful for the destruction of fortresses. We are destroying speculations and every lofty thing raised up *against the knowledge of God*, and we are taking every thought captive to the obedience of Christ . . ." (2 Corinthians 10:3-5 NAS, italics mine). Certainly Paul didn't mean the bookish knowledge of God, which we are to tuck into our minds for later reference, but the right-now-knowing of God, the Warrior beyond defeat! Paul advocated warfare against any and every fleshly incursion into our thoughts which might hinder our knowing God. That is the fleshly enemy tactic—prevent them from knowing Him because as they do, the holy evidence of Christ will overwhelm the twisted evidence of the flesh.

When the demolition derby begins banging around within, that's when God shows up in us. How? In the conflict, in light of the brawl, you (player #2) make a *thoughtful, believing choice*.

Galatians 5:16-17 tells us that living by the Spirit and being led by the Spirit means we will not succumb to the seduction of the flesh, we will not carry out its influential leading. Both the Spirit (player #1) and the flesh (player #3) *are influencers toward behavior*, and we are the recipients of that influence. The flesh attempts to influence you (player #2) in order that it may act through you expressing itself through your soul, the perceiver-expresser of your life. And what are its actions? How does it behave?

The acts *[the behavior]* of the flesh *[player #3]* are obvious *[and, oh, how you'll feel it!]*: sexual immorality, impurity and debauchery; idolatry and witchcraft; hatred, discord, jealousy, fits of rage, selfish ambition, dissensions, factions and envy; drunkenness, orgies, and the like. (Galatians 5:19-21 NAS, italics mine)

How 'bout that? Seen any of that stuff around your house lately? As you roll your eyes in recognition, consider: Who's acting? Who's misbehaving? Player #2? No. Player #3, Mr. Flesh, through you, player #2. It feels awful and it should—you lost the fight and the evidence is obvious . . . and twisted. You've been violated and abused.

Oh yes, in the end you're responsible. But did the real you, the actual you, the one born brand new, the new creation, son of God by nature *you* do it? No! It came *through you.* In the battle you fell under the influence, and you looked and did nasty, naughty stuff. But was it you? No, it came through you, and your perceiver-expresser, (your soul) put it on display.

That's why the apostle Paul said in his letter to the Roman church regarding foul, sinful behavior plaguing him: "Now if I do what I do not want to do, *it is no longer I who do it,* but it is sin living in me that does it" (Romans 7:20, italics mine). Paul knew what we must know: *there are three players in the drama.* Two players (#1 and #3) vie for influence leading to feelings and acts, one player (#2) follows the leader and out comes the action revealing the influence. See?

The apostle came to know that it wasn't up to him to produce feelings and desires leading to certain behaviors; *that wasn't and isn't the game!* Because we have been made vessels for God in which the demolition derby drama is at all times possible, <u>our role is *not* to produce what goes on inside but to choose sides and</u> <u>*give ourselves* to the Spirit.</u> He will then see to the outcome, and express Himself through us in godly feelings and behaviors. It's then that God's behavioral requirements are "fulfilled in us who do not walk according to the flesh *(player #3)* but according to the Spirit *(player #1)*" (Romans 8:4 NKJ, italics mine). It's a perfectly astounding fit!

And what can we (player #2) expect the influence of the Holy Spirit to be in the midst of the battle? What will the feelings and behavior coming through us look like and feel like if we offer ourselves to Him (player #1), right in that moment?

> But the fruit of the Spirit is love, joy, peace, patience, kindness, goodness, faithfulness, gentleness, and self-control; against such things there is no law. Now those who belong to Christ Jesus have crucified the flesh with its passions and desires. *If we live by the Spirit, let us also walk by the Spirit.* (Galatians 5:22-25 NAS, italics mine)

Can you imagine Him produced in you? His feelings, His ability, His likes manifested in you? What would be better than that? It feels right, too, and it should—you've been made for this.

How do we see Him formed in us? How may we have this delight? We'll look intently into that in a couple of chapters, but first it will be enormously helpful to see how it has been kept from you, how old and awful flesh behaviors have seemingly been resurrected and given new life. It's crazy, isn't it?

As a prelude to what's ahead, read a summarizing, three-sentence passage from know-it-all Paul:

> Therefore do not let sin reign in your mortal body so that you *[player #2]* obey its *[player #3]* evil desires. Do not offer the parts of your body to sin, as instruments of wickedness, but rather offer yourselves to God *[player #1]*, as those who have been brought from death to life; and offer the parts of your body to him as instruments of righteousness. For sin shall not be your master, because you are not under law, but under grace. (Romans 6:12-14, italics mine)

That's how grace works and it's especially effective for the demolition derby drama. You're set up for it and you're *better off than you think.*

been made free from our sin through one final sacrifice and have been given the righteousness of Another, our Savior, Jesus Christ! Now that's a ministry!

Read what the apostle Paul wrote, himself rather well acquainted with the two agreements God made for believers:

"He has made us competent as ministers of *a new covenant*— not of the letter but of the Spirit; for the letter kills, but the Spirit gives life. Now if the ministry that brought death, which was engraved in letters on stone, came with glory, so that the Israelites could not look steadily at the face of Moses because of its glory, fading though it was, will not the ministry of the Spirit be even more glorious? *If the ministry that condemns men is glorious, how much more glorious is the ministry that brings righteousness!* For what was glorious has no glory now in comparison with the surpassing glory. And if what was fading away came with glory, *how much greater is the glory of that which lasts!*" (2 Corinthians 3:6-11, italics mine).

So, what are you feeling right now? Stop and think. Stop. Think.

According to the Scriptures, He is *right now working* to convince you of what Jesus has given you and made you to be— righteous!

How much of your life have you spent wondering and worrying about your right doing and wrongdoing and how has it turned out? Have you felt the gift of God's freedom because of it or has it removed fear or dread? Has it ever, *ever* produced the real righteous behavior of Jesus, who is your life? Nah.

Now, I'm not saying you should give yourself a pass on lousy, sinful behavior or that God doesn't care about it anymore. That's not true. But what I am saying is that the way to good, acceptable behavior is through believing in what the Spirit is saying to you, *and it's far better than you suspect!*

As long as behavior is your focus, a standard of behavior has your attention and gets your motivation—that combo means your failure and condemnation—mark it down. And the Spirit's ministry to you will be to no avail because you'll believe He's entirely focused on your behavior, too. He isn't. It's a bad rap. Instead, He's looking at the behavior of Christ, and He knows you're in Him, in His behavior, in His history, and in His future!

And that makes something vital happen, something you may have been missing—it makes you delightfully *free.* "Where the Spirit of the Lord is, *there is freedom"* (2 Corinthians 3:17, italics mine).

If, in fact, Jesus set us free *so we would be and remain free* (see Galatians 5:1), then would it surprise you that it is now the ministry of the Spirit to remind you of that freedom—how good it is, how you got it, and what it entails? He isn't convicting you so you'll hang your head and engage in some anguished prayer of self-punishment or sorrowful sin offering. He already has the sin offering of Another! Yours isn't needed; in fact, it's an affront to His! Trusting in Jesus (in what He did concerning sin) is how you and I live by faith. And that's the way to live!

The chief effort of the devil, your cunning adversary, is and will be to disable the majesty of God's grace and gift to you. He cannot prevent your receiving it, but he will attempt to make it go unnoticed by you—and, therefore, ineffective.

Thank God, the Holy Spirit is the One who clues you in as to: who you are, upon whom you rely upon, how much you are loved, and how to live by faith. And He's the One who gives power to all of that. But if we believe He is all about something else—something less—we may avoid Him and attempt to go it alone. That's when ugly and old fleshly behaviors are seemingly resurrected and begin to plague us once again, no matter how hard we try to work against them.

When I'm delighting in the incredible grace of God to me in Christ and I reflect on how great is this new covenant made by the Father with Christ, the fruit of the Spirit is quickly in abundance—and I'm *not even working* at it. Believing in Him in me, I am free to be me, the me I am in reality, at the deepest point. I still get surprised by how great that real me is, the me in Christ, the one now sharing His nature, having been born entirely new through the work of the Spirit. In Him I'm a godly and free man! And so are you.

Sanctification is simply this, that believing in who Christ is for us, we offer ourselves to the Spirit throughout the day, His life and provision becoming ever more apparent as the days progress. Isn't that what you want?

And what is His intention? In addition to being on display in a holy vessel of His choosing and making, the Spirit intends that you and I should share in the very glory of God, now in us! Now—not just later.

> But we ought always to thank God for you, brothers loved by the Lord, because from the beginning God chose you to be saved through the sanctifying work of the Spirit and through belief in the truth. He called you to this through our gospel, *that you might share in the glory of our Lord Jesus Christ.* (2 Thessalonians 2:13-14, italics mine)

Wow. What a plan. Have the odds of offering yourself to Him gone up? He's great to have around, great to have within, great to know! He's not the heavy you may have thought He was.

My hope—my prayer—is that you, too, will enjoy a fresh breeze of awareness and subsequent confidence in the Spirit now in you. Feeling condemned? It's not from Him. Feeling separated from Him? It's not true. Feeling particularly filthy today? That's not true, either. Your flesh, despicable as ever, may have led you down the sad trail of temptation, there to make you stumble and to torment you, even holding out the evidence in support of the charges of the Accuser.

But the *real you*, the you God made at *new birth*, remains intact, unaltered, and radiant in the radiance of Another, waiting to be stimulated through the sanctifying, convincing work of the Holy Spirit.

So, feeling convicted? Me too. Isn't it great?

Chapter Seven

Hitting My Pause Button

Since we live by the Spirit, let us keep in step
with the Spirit. Let us not become conceited, pro-
voking and envying each other.
(Galatians 5:25-26)

Many years ago a couple of us were trying to impress the same girl. We were each about thirteen and were making awkward attempts at figuring out how to get what we wanted in life. My competition thought he could out-clever me, but she laughed a lot more following my comments than his. I won. Of course, he proceeded to beat me up. Oops. I hadn't counted on that but that's life. Since we all lived on the same street, they could see me cower all the way home.

For years I learned to live as best I could around that guy—*way around*. For the most part we were civil to each other, but whenever my bully was near, I could feel myself shrinking inside. I hated that feeling. I did my best to deal with it by looking confident and assured on the outside while making my way in the opposite direction.

At a large reunion party some fifteen years later, a group of us were discussing what we were doing with our lives when we were joined by my bully. Around the group we went, and as doctor this, accountant that, salesperson this, manager that elaborated on how we were doing with our dreams, it came to me.

When I said, "I'm a Youth Pastor," my bully scowled and asked, "Is that it!" And I felt that old shrink all over again. He'd won. After that I wasn't the same at the party. On the whole two-hour drive home, I lamented to God that I felt ashamed of my title and life. Well, God loves me and thinks highly of me, and He calmed and soothed me all the way home, securing me—it turned out to be a great drive.

The very next night I had to return to that same town. Pulling into one of a hundred gas stations, I parked next to the pump and noticed my bully pulling in right next to me. "*Dear God,*" I thought. He got out and asked the strangest question: "Hey, Ralph! What's with all this Christian stuff, anyway?"

My first thought was, "It's my time for *revenge!*" I began to beat him with the Gospel. In clear terms so he wouldn't miss his beating, I took him on a tour of the Gospel only so I could tell him where he was sure to go. As the heat got hotter and my old resentment made me feel like Mike Tyson, in my mind I was suddenly interrupted by the Holy Spirit. "You don't like him, do you?" came His question. Suddenly staring into space, I paused and was momentarily silenced. Finally I thought in response— No. Not at all. And the Spirit said, "But I do. Would you like my love for him?" Somehow, someway, I responded—Yes.

Immediately everything within me changed—I loved my bully! I found not one fault with him and had not one bit of resentment, I was so filled with love. My eyes spilling over with tears, I said, "The reason I am a Christian is I know for sure that Jesus loves me and that has changed everything; I cannot live without Him. He loves you amazingly and longs to show you what He is like toward you. His love for you is intense and when you are ready to ask Him to show you what He is like toward you, He will. You've only to ask."

His head cocked to one side, his eyes and mouth wide open, my bully stammered, "Uh, I've never heard anything like that in my life. Thank you. Thank you."

That night at the gas station, I felt and knew the love of God for someone I thought I despised. There had been no strategy for it, no working it up, and no earning it. But the One who lives in me had something in mind, and He convinced me to say yes to His love. Frankly, the last thing I wanted was love for my bully, and probably the last thing he wanted—neither of us liked each other! Yet God in me produced what He thought and felt and I was deeply involved. Oddly, it felt like me too.

That was almost twenty years ago, and while I haven't seen my bully since, the pursuit of my life has never been the same.

(About a year ago I learned that my bully, after making a notable mess of things, had become a Christian and had begun a ministry to inner-city youth. I guess God really does love him!) From that day to this, my primary passion has been to know Christ in me in such a way that He might live evidently through me. That one desire has provided the direction for my life, moving me from place to place, from singleness to marriage, and from ministry to ministry.

In order to find Him in me, two things had to be true which we looked at in the last chapter: first, I had to believe He was there; second, I had to look for Him. And now I would add a third aspect: *I have to momentarily do nothing* . . . and that's not easy. I'll give you an example and then I'll explain.

When Jesus walked amongst us, sickness was at least as frightening as it is today and usually quicker to cause death. Remember the men who dug through a roof, lowering their sick friend into the house below so Jesus could heal him? If you or someone you loved were sick and you knew a way back to health, you wouldn't hesitate to take advantage. So it shouldn't be surprising that people who knew Jesus would clamor for His attention concerning a sick relative.

We find another such situation in the book of John:

> Now a man named Lazarus was sick. He was from Bethany, the village of Mary and her sister Martha. This Mary, whose brother Lazarus now lay sick, was the same one who poured perfume on the Lord and wiped his feet with her hair. So the sisters sent word to Jesus, "Lord, the one you love is sick. "When he heard this, Jesus said, "This sickness will not end in death. No, it is for God's glory so that God's Son may be glorified through it. "Jesus loved Martha and her sister and Lazarus. Yet when he heard that Lazarus was sick, he stayed where he was two more days. (John 11:1-6)

What did Jesus do when the sisters presented their concern to Him? What were His actions toward those He loved? He did nothing! In fact, Jesus remained where He was for a couple more days. Why?

Even as Jesus lived fully as a human being, He lived day to day, moment by moment fully dependent upon the Father for direction and provision (see John 5:19, 30). He didn't do a thing without Him! And so, no matter how briefly, *Jesus paused.* And in that moment of delay, the Father communicated with the Son that He should do nothing because the Father had something planned for glory; Jesus should wait upon Him because the sickness wasn't the earthly end for Lazarus. (To see how the rest of the story came out, read John 11:11-44.)

Jesus' pause (His momentary do-nothing) was a pause of faith, and that's why He knew to do nothing after it. He believed the Father would speak to Him because the Father had a supreme interest in the situation, and Jesus believed He would hear Him. In faith (*"Do nothing just now . . ."*), Jesus spoke to the sister's messenger, and free from the demanding urgency of the moment, got on with the next issue at hand.

If I had been there, I might have thought, What! How can you have no concern? How can you not do something—and these are your friends! And look around! Everyone's watching! What a perfect time to do something for the glory of God and you do nothing? I can't believe it!

Jesus *was* doing something for the glory of God, and we would do well to live after the same manner as He. As Jesus did, hitting our personal pause button in the face of urgent needs and desires means we believe *something else defines reality and that Someone else* may well have something He'd like to do. That's faith! While it can be very difficult in the face of pressing needs and desires, pausing on purpose is one of the most significant points of faith I know. If you believe that God lives in you, knows everything—*everything*—and that He can do something about everything, why not take a moment, a fraction of a second, to look and listen for Him? This is how to get a healthy and godly perceiver-expresser!

A faith-filled delay is a terrific blow against the devil and the flesh, which would love to circumnavigate God in you by seducing you to something *reasonable* or *responsible* in the press of the moment. Do anything—*anything*—but pause *on purpose,* listening for the Holy Spirit who lives in you. Think of the threat that is to all things demonic! By a simple delay, we can know God and follow His leading, whether that's to say something, say nothing, do something, do nothing, or simply to hear Him or share in His feelings. When we wait expectantly for Him, we, who are so often transfixed and motivated by all things temporal and visible, bring great glory and honor "to the King *eternal, immortal, invisible* . . ." (1 Timothy 1:17). This is how to know what's *really* going on in light of present circumstances, this is how to be free of the temporal demand (Quick! Do something!) because you're sowing toward eternity! If God knows what will happen before it happens, why not seek His counsel? Here's why: we've been taking another route.

As we saw in Chapter Four, the flesh has long offered us a way to get through life, to get what we need, to look good in front of others, to avoid what we don't want and, for most, it has become normal—living by the flesh is how we live. But Paul wrote of another way to live, a normal way for those born of the Spirit—the highest way. "I consider everything a loss compared to the surpassing greatness of *knowing Christ Jesus* my Lord, for whose sake I have lost all things. I consider them rubbish, that I may gain Christ" (Philippians 3:8, italics mine). Wow! He really meant it. That's what happens when, resisting the press of the moment, resisting the urge to give an answer that makes us look good, resisting the demand to come up with something clever or cute, we momentarily do nothing, we pause with an inner question, What are your thoughts, Jesus? What do you feel about this? Is there something you would like to do? I have faith in you, my Lord.

If our highest goal is to know God right in front of people and situations, then we will resist the urge and offering of the flesh. If it isn't and if we don't look toward the invisible world, then most of our efforts will go toward adjusting to this visible world, to make it a better place, to get along comfortably within it, to keep ourselves as happy and fulfilled as we can, and to assist others toward the same ends by the same means. And yet, from God's perspective we may be failing, unintentionally living by the influence of the flesh—life without the life of God.

Why would any Christian live under the influence of the flesh? The answer to that question is essentially that he or she doesn't believe in the incredible extent of God's grace to us in Christ, and so lives in order to get and manage life by other means.

That's no crime and we're not stupid. Most of our life has sent us the message that God is unreliable concerning our needs and desires, so *we'd* better control it. If you want to avoid rejection, do this. If you want to steer clear of failure, do that. If you want to be popular, do this. If you want to get ahead, do that. Control *yourself* and you will control *life.*

That's the bait. Swallow it and you'll learn to live to have control rather than live to have Him.

The problem we're having is that we're confusing the life God produces with the life we can have and the two are different. One kind of life is our life*style*. It can be had by choosing the right techniques, living by the right principles, and by offering ourselves to the best efforts. Control *yourself* and you will control life. The other kind of life is the life which moves us from the inside toward the outside. It can be found by believing and offering yourself to the Holy Spirit, who will produce in you what God is like.

But if we don't do that, we will live in order to find the just-right prescription of how to win at life. That will always result in failure and frustration for the sons of God who will have exchanged knowing God in life for control of life—life by the Spirit for life by the flesh. Fortunately, believers so living will eventually feel uncomfortable, unnatural, and out of step with the Spirit because they've been taken hostage to something not at all like them.

So, how does the flesh look? How does it get my attention? We know that throughout our life things have happened which induced us to believe the lie that God was not capable for us or that He wasn't reliable, and so we chose the avenue offered by the flesh. You and I will know that avenue as something which feels relatively secure (a way to get what we want or avoid what we don't want) but it will be flesh, all the same.

To help you see the avenues of your flesh, I've made up some names for those common ways of living to control life which unintentionally sacrifice knowing God . . . and sacrifice *life* from God. See if you recognize how the flesh has led you away from knowing God by offering you control. Keep in mind that this fleshly activity is not you, but something which influences and drives you—you don't want it anymore.

Chicken flesh. In most every conflict, you quickly feel like running away—like getting out of there. Life as you like it feels threatened, and the best course of action is to leave. If you must remain, then you'd better walk on egg shells because you just don't know what might happen. Go chicken and run. I have this flesh. Now, sometimes you *should* leave, especially if you truly are at risk. But this flesh suggests an exodus course for life whenever a decent argument or stressful circumstance occurs, not just on occasion but usually. Sowing to the Spirit and listening for Him, by pausing to offer yourself to Him, isn't on the menu at all. But it could be.

After returning from a long day of substitute teaching, Sarah was particularly annoyed—I could feel it. No longer was she bothered only by unruly kids, but she was bothered by traffic on the way home, by unhelpful teaching assistants, by ill-fitting clothing, and by the weather. Feeling her irritation, this thought presented itself to me: "Don't say anything. Just quietly walk away and let her blow off steam. You *know* how she gets. This tension in the room is a bad feeling, isn't it? Walk away and you will feel better." Frankly, Sarah doesn't lash out at me, she doesn't take it out on me, and I'm not at all at risk! But in the conflict, my flesh offers me a way of living, which if followed, will eventually allow for it to behave through me. In the short run, it feels like I escape. In the long run, I take a beating when the flesh, having led me successfully away from the Spirit, behaves through me.

Well, that day, while feeling every bit of the conflict, *I paused* and offered myself to the Spirit. Immediately I heard the Spirit say, "You are well. Go and rescue your wife." Feeling better, but hearing nothing more, I approached Sarah and said, "I love you." Remaining open to the Spirit, confident He would shape my words, I continued by saying, "You have been roughed-up by the world today, which can never accurately identify you. Always it will resist who you are in Christ, never reflecting back the honor and glory due you. If you're tired and worn out it's not because you have failed, it's because you've been in a struggle with a worldly system which makes little room for you. According to God, you're the best there is in this world, even as it rejects you. You're wonderful."

Immediately she was revived. By my sowing to the Holy Spirit, He produced in me *faithfulness* (I believed He was in me and that He would do something for Sarah from there), He produced in me *self-control* and *peace* (I didn't turn chicken), *gentleness* (I didn't scold her, or tell her to "Change your attitude!"), and *love*. Holding one another, we knew who we were—the sacred sons of God. And we loved! And we had *life*.

Brute flesh. This fleshly driven person gets along in life by snuffing out disagreements and by abruptly ending dialogue with "I don't want to hear it anymore! That's it! We're done!" Leaning toward the other party with eyes narrowed and fists clenched, brute flesh demands, "Got it? Are we *clear*?" which means, "It's my way or the highway—you choose!" This believer has learned to rule the roost by inducing fear in those around him. He walks around with an invisible line drawn in the sand; cross him and he will cross you. Everyone knows Mr. Brute is not to be messed with because what he gives in return is way too dangerous. To be clear, this fleshly led person doesn't just rarely lose it and brute his way to a conclusion he wants—he does it regularly, for it has become a way of navigating life. It isn't him but he doesn't know it, having found no better way to live. But there is a better way and a pause will help him find it.

Nascar flesh. What works for this fleshly driven Christian is life at 160 miles per hour. Pit stops are very rare and, even then, work is part of lunch, business part of breakfast, and strategy a part of most every relationship. A key sign that *Nascar flesh* is in operation is that this person feels truly guilty when sickness lays him out, incapacitating him. Waiting upon the Holy Spirit and sowing toward Him doesn't fit with the need for speed driving this fleshly believer. Resting in Christ is a foreign language. He can be helped not by telling him to slow down or by waving him into the pits (he's liable to run you over!) but by asking him questions: "What do you think God's opinion is on this matter?" "What are God's feelings for you right now?" If he cannot answer (he's going 160!), the Holy Spirit will later bring to his mind the questions you've posted there.

Unfortunately, and because these people get a lot done, they are rarely helped. Instead, they burn out. The way to wellness is not to manage themselves better (they'll do it as fast as they can) but to believe God lives in them and wants to provide from there. Only that pleasure will induce this driven believer to slow down.

→ *Nike flesh.* "Just do it" is this person's motto; "Git 'er done," a close second. While speed is not their issue, task accomplishment is—they live for it and that's the problem. They have allowed measurable accomplishment to take the place of knowing God. They feel better only when their tasks are completed to their satisfaction, and nothing brings them more peace than that. Their prayer life is overwhelmingly themed with sincere requests about what to do. The flesh has sown a lie to them that God is to be known because He is useful; He always has a plan to make life work. If they can get to Him, He is sure to tell them what it is and that's what's most important. But it isn't.

These believers are often employed as administrators and project managers—they're terrific at getting a job done. They're not so terrific at relaxing with people. They'll fidget and wonder what task could be getting done instead . . . and drift away to do it. Instead of commanding them to "Sit down and spend some time with me, Martha!" you can help them by sowing to the Spirit and perhaps asking a question or two. "What do you think God is thinking right now? If He were to suddenly show up, what would he want for you?" They may initially feel uncomfortable with your questions, but when they know you're not trying to corral and break them but rather usher them toward life by the Spirit, they will begin to pay attention. Remember, *Nike flesh* people are God's project—not ours.

→ *Cavalry flesh.* These believers are driven away from knowing and relying upon the Holy Spirit in them by the lure to rescue. They live by the trumpet call of the cavalry and always have a fast horse waiting. Every need they hear about beckons them to devise a way to bring comfort quickly. Any emotional pain or unresolved relational mess launches them toward resolution. They must help you be well because wellness is everything! After all, isn't God the Great Physician? Unfortunately, they can interrupt a work of the Spirit who has something deeper and more lasting in mind than a simple surface healing. For those with Cavalry flesh, sanctification is less about being genuinely transformed in cooperation with the Holy Spirit as it is about feeling better about oneself. When these habit-formed Christians hear the trumpet call of need, they must resist the fleshly demand by pausing and offering themselves to the Spirit. Their thrill in life will be found in knowing Him who is, indeed, the Rescuer. They will love being included in the big picture of His rescue and will learn to relax in light of His plan and ability.

Sunny Day flesh. If you're driven by the belief that life is only good when everything is positive, you may have *Sunny Day flesh.* Frankly, everything in my life isn't good, everything isn't positive, and I'm not always encouraged—that's a fact and it's okay! It's normal. However, believers driven by this flesh have always got to put a positive spin on everything; it's how they've learned to live. These are good, yet fleshly, people to visit (they're your cheerleaders!) but no fun to live with because they'll attempt to orchestrate you to be good and happy at all times too. If you're having a marginally bad moment and would like to know Jesus in it, they will overwhelm you with optimism, driving you up and out of your downer day. They must have everything and everyone "just right" in order to move ahead and live—that's the lie. Even though Jesus said that, like Him, we would be well acquainted with suffering, there is little place for that with those of this type of flesh.

So when trial or difficulty is presented to them, life is managed by staying upbeat and positive, not by pausing and turning toward the Holy Spirit who has much to say and do for them. See the twist? Nothing is wrong with being positive unless it becomes a manner of life, keeping you from knowing the life of God within. When once these believers are helped, they will have the load of the world taken from their shoulders (after all, they've been responsible to make it happy) and will, instead, find the joy of Christ produced in them. You want to be around them when that happens because it is a delight to behold!

IRYW flesh. This brand of flesh ("I'm Right, You're Wrong") constructs for the afflicted the notion that being right is everything—it motivates them. They read their Bibles not so much to know the One it speaks about, but to be right in doctrine, correct in discussion, free from wrong, the scary opposite of right. When once an opinionated discussion blows in, they navigate it with "Yeah, but . . ." and "Well, but . . ." and even "True, but . . ." all to show fellow conversationalists that they aren't as right as he is. In light of how right he is, they're wrong. The way to help them is not to show them they're wrong (though you may be tempted!) but to not play that game. When they see how this fleshly lure affects them (they're often identified as arrogant and prideful), keeping them from the delight of the Holy Spirit, they will quiet down and not have to end every conversation with a victory. Instead, they will be having Him who is right, and that will be sufficient and satisfying. With an intentional pause, He will provide for them what their flesh has been seductively offering: peace, comfort, and security.

Whiner flesh. For some of us life has sent the message that if we whine and whimper we get what we want. Whine and we get fed. Whimper and we don't get punished. Whine and we get noticed. Whimper and we get sympathy. If this fleshly course of action has succeeded for long, evidence of its effectiveness makes it a challenge to take another course of action. When a whine works, pausing instead to think of the Spirit seems ineffective and it is if getting what we want is more important than knowing God! That's the trick. Smacking a "No whiners allowed!" sticker on their forehead doesn't work; it will only frustrate them because it does nothing toward the Spirit who is having the conflict within.

Rather than interpret lots of situations as worthy of a whine, these fleshly Christians need to see the conflict within for what it is. "I want something and I'm afraid God won't give it to me— He is insufficient here. So, this is an alternate course to get what I want." When they see how ugly that belief is, they will be helped toward turning away from the avenue of the flesh toward the Holy Spirit . . . and that whine you've been hearing will be greased.

Detective flesh. These flesh-driven people come at you with all the warmth of a microscope. They over-examine most everything, including you and everything you say–they make you uncomfortable. It's not so much that they want to get to know you as it is that they want to find something, something they suspect you're hiding. Not only do they think that everyone is an unsolved mystery, with dangerous twists and turns and hidden secrets which, if revealed might shock the world, but they think everyone is *their* mystery to solve. So they dig for clues.

Detective flesh people will ask probing questions and then draw conclusions about you, sometimes right in front of you, as if you were no longer there. "So, then, Ralph's a twin and a middle child, which means he's a peace-loving negotiator, doesn't like strife and wants to be liked. Most likely a sanguine, too, so he loves a crowd . . . hmm."

Through the years of their experience they have come to believe that knowing as much as they can about everyone and everything will keep them safe. Knowledge means control and that's a powerful motivator. They want to know every angle on everyone that could possibly hurt or disappoint them–make sure everything is out of everyone's closet. They'll drag it out if they need to. Frankly, they may have good reason, having been surprised and wounded in the past. You shouldn't be quick to blame them (or others) for falling to a seemingly advantageous way of life offered by the flesh. They dislike the unknown because it may hurt them. Often these believers will be at least somewhat correct in their assessment of people and that can be valuable.

But where they're trapped is revealed by how bound they are to making assessments and how often they keep people away from their heart. *Detective flesh* people seal off their hearts as though dealing with a crime scene—wearing gloves and masking their faces when interacting with others. They may touch you but they won't get close. They won't remove their protective coverings unless they find something better fitting— the safety of the Holy Spirit who knows everything about everyone already. He is certain to alert them and clue them in when needed and, in Him, they will have what they have been seeking—*security*.

Frankly, there are many more! *Martyr flesh* ("If I don't do it, nobody will!" motivates these fleshly believers' resentment-filled days); *Octopus flesh* (they look for the angle which gives them the advantage in everything); *Scrooge flesh* (you can figure that one out); *Magnifier flesh* (everything is made out to be worse than it actually is); *Fixer-upper flesh* (nearly everyone they meet begs the just-right touch which will make them just right for the marketplace); *Loner flesh* (these believe and act on the lie that there's no place in the body of Christ for them); *Barbie flesh* (unless they look their best at all times, something tragic will happen—life is a parade); *Linear flesh* (life is just waiting for them to finally get it right. Once they do, *then* they will really be living . . . they may not know God, but they'll be living), and on and on it goes.

When bringing some of these fleshly lures to light at seminars, invariably the audience begins to see how their particular flesh has kept them from sowing to the Spirit by offering another way . . . and they've seen the results. They haven't found God particularly satisfying nor capable. When they begin making up their own labels for the flesh, I know they've got it; they see it and the secret lure away from the Holy Spirit has been revealed as worthless tin.

I should hasten to add that some of these characteristics can be a part of our natural, God-given personality. Some of us are simply wired by God to notice people. And sometimes you just have to do or say something immediately, wondering later if what you did or said was by the Spirit. Sometimes that's simply the way it is, and it's okay; God works in us that way too. (And remember, this isn't a way for you to *finally* do things *just right* with God—*Hooray!* Now He'll *notice* me! It is another way to know and enjoy Him and He'll be glorified in that.) It's just that most of the time we're not waiting at all, but rushing into the conflict and into the scene too soon—wanting and working to get something done. That's the lure and we miss the Holy Spirit because we're after the fleshly bait.

Doing absolutely nothing is not the solution; neither is ignoring the lure! Offering yourself to the Spirit when the lure drags by your face is the course you want because life is with Him! It is a new way to live, to be sure, and growing into it most likely won't happen by this time tomorrow. But over time it will happen because it is *the* way—He will bring you to it.

> But now, by dying to what once bound us, we have been released from the law so that we serve in the new way of the Spirit, and not in the old way of the written code. (Romans 7:6)

It should be evident that those of us under the influence of the flesh may look particularly bad, or we may look particularly *good*. And that's a more difficult thing to see and a more difficult thing from which to turn. But it's just as fleshly, just as foreign, and just as dangerous. I might appear to be the most faithful church attender in the world, but I might be doing it because I fear God will bless me *only if I do* and not at all if I don't. So I go . . . under the influence. I don't mean to imply that regular church attendance is a bad thing; it isn't! It's just that under the influence of the flesh, it becomes *the thing*. Going to church gets the greater emphasis—not knowing God. The evidence might include condemning thoughts and feelings toward those who fail to attend as regularly or I might frequently and strongly encourage others to attend as the solution to their lack of blessing or, perhaps, I take a leadership position on the "Let's-get-the-church-to-church-on-time-every-Sunday" committee. I'm active but I'm nevertheless fleshly.

Under this influence, I'm not free to ask and trace out the godly and good reasons for going to church, sowing to the Spirit who might lead me here or there, finding His gifts in me to do this or that, and helping me to live by faith. Instead, I'm captive to what looks right and to what ought to be, and that's where the flesh is found.

Fleshly activity is not you, but something which influences and drives you–it should be much more evident having read this chapter. Should we now run off and point out each other's flesh types? Be very careful because the flesh may be motivating you to do that and not the Spirit. It's not hard to imagine the fun you could have with this new knowledge. That could become as fleshly a lure as anything else—resist the nibble by pausing to offer yourself to the Holy Spirit. "Since we live by the Spirit, let us keep in step with the Spirit. Let us not become conceited, provoking and envying each other"(Galatians 5:25-26).

The flesh is not you, but it would like to provide a way for you to look. If you follow its tin lure of promised control, it will behave through you. You know how that will look and feel, and you want to be done with it. Now that you know better, now that you believe life by the Spirit is both possible and desirable, chances are good you'll refuse the bait and go for the Spirit. All it takes is an expectant pause.

And that's good news.

Chapter Eight

Doin' the Monster Mash

*Does God give you his Spirit and work miracles
among you because you observe the law, or
because you believe what you heard?*
(Galatians 3:5)

*Always go to other people's funerals, otherwise
they won't come to yours. Yogi Berra*

About a dozen of us from my church were squirming uncomfortably in our seats. Gathered together with hundreds of others for a men's retreat at a Christian camp, the speaker was really giving it to us. Lord knows we deserved it.

"How many of you pray every day with your wife? How many? Why not? Don't you know you're inviting the legions of hell into your house? There is no excuse, especially when so much is at risk, so much is at stake! You must pray with your wife every day! Every day! Ehhhhhhhhhhhhhhhvvvrrreeeeeeee-eeeeeeeeeee day! Until you do, you can't expect God to honor you! You must commit to it, before the Lord you must commit to praying with your wife every day!"

A week or two later, I took an informal poll. When I asked how their prayer commitment was going, every head dropped. Though all of us agreed with the speaker that we should pray every day with our wives, none of us had followed through.

"I meant to," one said, "I even put it in my day timer. But it just didn't seem to work out."

Another said, "I've been feeling guilty ever since." (Nods from all the men.) "I guess I'm just not a prayer warrior . . . Seems like it has affected all of my prayer life."

One more said, "I thought I could do it—I've wanted to! But it seems like the way I once was before I accepted Jesus gets back into the picture and messes me up. I thought all that was buried and gone . . ."

We were not a happy bunch.

Do you ever behave in the poor way you did before you became a Christian? Do you ever struggle with the same temptations you did before your new life in Christ? No matter how much you pray and fight against them, do some of those old ugly desires and thoughts rise from the dead and put you to shame?

Me too.

If that old nasty "I" was crucified with Christ, then what beckons to the seeming graveyard of my life, inducing the monster in me to rise from the dead? What is it which so stimulates the flesh that I cannot resist its bidding?

I remember as a small boy dancing to Bobby Pickett's classic, "The Monster Mash." It wasn't well choreographed but it sure was fun, and I've danced to it every October since. Know how it goes?

> I was working in the lab late one night
> When my eyes beheld an eerie sight
> For my monster from his slab began to rise
> And suddenly to my surprise

> He did the mash
> He did the monster mash
> The monster mash
> It was a graveyard smash
> He did the mash
> It caught on in a flash
> He did the mash
> He did the monster mash

> From my laboratory in the castle east
> To the master bedroom where the vampires feast
> The ghouls all came from their humble abodes
> To get a jolt from my electrodes

Look again at Romans 7:5, "For when we were controlled by the sinful nature, *the sinful passions aroused by the law* were at work in our bodies, so that we bore fruit for death" (NAS, italics mine).

What electrodes make the monster mash? What is it which stimulates the flesh? Rules. Must dos. Must not dos. Laws arouse sin.

So think about it. How does the devil fool the believer? What's his tactic to get the believer to stumble, frustrate him, and get him to fail? He gets him to live by rules. The flesh or the devil will suggest something like, "You know how you've been doing lately . . . you've got to do better. You'd better get with it." Convinced, we nod in agreement, rededicate our lives to God, begin again to focus upon what we're supposed to do and not do, and we pray prayers like this: "Lord, help me to do the things you want me to do." In other words, "Help me keep your rules."

Turn up the music because you're about to do the mash— welcome to the flesh! There is nothing so effective in showing people what failure and sin is and how it works, as the pronouncement of rules and laws. God intended it to be so. Paul writes, "What shall we say, then? Is the law sin? Certainly not! Indeed I would not have known what sin was *except* through the law. For I would not have known what coveting really was if the law had not said, 'Do not covet'" (Romans 7:7, italics mine).

I can tell you, it works! It's perfectly effective! Why then would we think we can now live by rules in such a way as to break the intended effect? "But sin, seizing the opportunity *afforded by the commandment,* produced in me every kind of covetous desire. For apart from law, sin is dead" (Romans 7:8, italics mine). Did you get that last sentence? Turn it around and it would read, "Sin is dead without laws to invigorate it." The very power of sin is the law (see 1 Corinthians 15:56).

And we try to live by it? That's crazy. No, that's demonic.

Any approach to Christian living that *focuses* and depends upon keeping rules as the means of experiencing spiritual growth or victory binds you to sin because you're arousing the wrong self, the pretender self, the *monster!* Each time you tack up a new pledge of obedience on the wall of your mind, an assault has already begun. "*I promise,*" "*I commit,*" are the well-intentioned responses to the suggestions of the flesh inviting us to a battle it is sure to win. That's why it is so quick and happy to respond to your promises. "Thank you, Ralph, for calling and inviting me to dance. I'll take the lead now . . ." And here comes life without the life of God.

In chapter 5 we looked at how that dance will go with the flesh in the lead. ". . . Sexual immorality, impurity and debauchery; idolatry and witchcraft; hatred, discord, jealousy, fits of rage, selfish ambition, dissensions, factions and envy; drunkenness, orgies, and the like . . ." (Galatians 5:19-21). How ugly that dance makes the captured Christian look, a noble one being pushed and abused all over the dance floor of their life!

Have you seen it? Have you danced the terrible dance? I have too. It helps to know *it's not your dance* and you're not in the lead, and it will help to know how to take the lead and really live and dance the way you were redesigned. It'll be beautiful! It's your design and it's your destiny, "Thanks be to God! He gives us the victory through our Lord Jesus Christ" (1 Corinthians 15:57).

There's a new way to live, a new way to dance that you'll love and which is in keeping with who and what you are; it's your new normal, the new way of the Spirit. Jesus completed and canceled the former covenant, making it obsolete and releasing us from its harsh instruction so we may live by faith in Him (see Galatians 3:23-25). Your new way to live is by the grace and leading of the Holy Spirit now in you, and while that takes some getting used to, there's nothing better!

Watchman Nee wrote, "Grace means that God does something for me; law means that I do something for God. God has certain holy and righteous demands which He places upon me; that is law. Now if law means that God requires something of me for their fulfillment, then deliverance from law means that He no longer requires that from me, but Himself provides it. Law implies that God requires me to do something for Him; deliverance from law implies that He exempts me from doing it, and that in grace He does it Himself. I need do nothing for God: that is deliverance from law."

You died to the laws that you might live to Jesus. Fantastic! Law keeping might hold out the promise of godly living and you might for a time pull it off. But law keeping and perfect behavior will never produce intimacy with God. Instead it will put you back into the prison of failure with Paul and return you to a fearful relationship with God as "the warden." Intimacy with your loving Father will lead to His behavior coming through you, His son.

And that's the way to dance.

Therefore, there is now no condemnation for those who are in Christ Jesus, because through Christ Jesus the law of the Spirit of life set me free from the law of sin and death. For what the law was powerless to do in that it was weakened by the sinful nature, God did by sending his own Son in the likeness of sinful man to be a sin offering. And so he condemned sin in sinful man, in order that the righteous requirements of the law might be fully met in us, who do not live according to the sinful nature but according to the Spirit. (Romans 8:1-4)

Chapter Nine

Cleaning Up Toxic Relationships

But now, by dying to what once bound us, we have been released from the law so that we serve in the new way of the Spirit, and not in the old way of the written code. (Romans 7:6)

If Jesus wanted to tag along and interact with everyone you know and everyone you meet, would you be encouraged to invite Him? Would you trust Him to talk with and treat each person just the way He wanted? The night before your first day together, would you be excited? What do you think your day would be like? What if you could live like that every day, with Jesus as your tagalong? Would you have to worry about how you would treat everyone? Would you be concerned with whether or not your relational skills were sufficient for each relationship and every meeting?

What's to worry? You'd have Jesus with you and however your encounters went, people would think of you in relation to Him. Frankly, He would soon become the headliner and you the tagalong. You wouldn't mind, would you? It would sure mean life from a different angle, wouldn't it?

I ask all these questions because I want to get your hopes up and prepare you for a royal burden-lifting. Because you're maturing in Christ and learning to live by the Spirit, you should expect it. Perhaps, far back on the shelf of expectation, you've long ago left any real hope of finding rest as a direct result of your life in Christ. It's time to take up your hope, dust it off, and have a new look.

In our day one of the biggest concerns we have is how to successfully navigate relationships. Think of the books you've read, the sermons you've heard, the rules at work, even the classroom time devoted to how we're to treat others and you will see how deeply involved we are with relationships. Our ability is almost constantly on trial, the demand to perform is around every corner, and a report card is offered at nearly every meeting. We're focused on relationships.

So tell me, how do you do with relationships? What kind of people get under your skin and what are you doing about that? Are you submitting to leaders from your heart? Are you treating your spouse the way you're supposed to? Do you think of yourself as too blunt or too reserved? Too shy or too outgoing? Too quick to commit or too slow? Probably you've thought of all these things because you estimate yourself by how you do with people, like the rest of us. It judges our days. Our interaction with others is the white-hot spotlight on the stage of our life and everybody's looking; everybody sees.

Because of this audience, the pressure to come up with the just-right performance might well be the lure that makes actors of us while robbing us of the heart for what we're doing. And it might be the single most effective lure cast through this world which draws us away from life by the Spirit and knowing Jesus throughout the day—right in front of each other.

I think the most satisfying course for relationships has been taken from us, particularly for marriage (happily recommended by the apostle Paul). At first reading it will seem terribly irresponsible. It always does when I read it as the first Scripture to begin a Christian marriage seminar or retreat: "What I mean, brothers, is that the time is short. *From now on those who have wives should live as if they had none . . .*" (1 Corinthians 7:29, italics mine).

Silence. Every eye is on me. Immediately, I've got their attention. True, some are bothered with me and nearly all are confused but they're listening. Most don't think it's in the Bible, but I believe it is one of the most important introductions for Christian living found in Scripture.

Got a wife? Live as though you didn't. Just got a husband? Keep living the way you were before you did. That's best. That'll work. "Got it everyone? Okay, let's go *home.*"

"How does this square with marriage?" their faces question. "How can we live like that and have a good marriage?" Good questions—ones the Holy Spirit wanted to address to the Corinthians through Paul because something other than a good marriage was His first goal, something which would be the greatest influence for marriage and all of our relationships—making good ones possible.

Written to the love-confused Corinthians, 1 Corinthians 7:29 is the beginning of Paul's summary of what to do if married. For the Christian, the number one problem with marriage is not finances, it's not communication, it's not what to do about children; the problem with marriage is that you're *married*. Once you are, you're going to act like it and work like it and think like it. Worse, you're going to be concerned about it and really devoted, and that's no good because you're about to be divided. That's a killer—*don't let it happen.*

Because time was short for the Corinthians (and is for all of us), Paul continues in verse thirty by writing that, "…those who mourn, *[should live]* as if they did not; those who are happy, as if they were not; those who buy something, as if it were not theirs to keep; those who use the things of the world, as if not engrossed in them. *For this world in its present form is passing away*" (1 Corinthians 7:30-31, italics mine).

The world we live in is transitory, it's terminal but we're not. We're not of this world and we don't live for it—we live for something else and that's what's threatened.

Continuing in verse thirty-two, Paul writes, *"I would like you to be free from concern.* An unmarried man is concerned about the Lord's affairs—how he can please the Lord. But a married man is concerned about the affairs of this world—how he can please his wife—*and his interests are divided.* An unmarried woman or virgin is concerned about the Lord's affairs: Her aim is to be devoted to the Lord in both body and spirit. But a married woman is concerned about the affairs of this world—how she can please her husband" (1 Corinthians 7:32-34, italics mine).

What's the problem? Marriage and our concern for it! Paul doesn't want that for us because it draws us too deeply into the affairs and distractions of this world, dividing us between the world we're from and the world we're in. That's a terrible way to live! He writes, *"I am saying this for your own good*, not to restrict you, but that you may live in a right way *in undivided devotion to the Lord"* (1 Corinthians 7:35, italics mine).

Marriage (and all relationships, for that matter) may easily become the thief of singular devotion to Jesus. That's Paul's startling point. The conclusion he gives to the Corinthians is that the right way to live—the Christian way—is in *undivided devotion to Jesus*. That's how you and I live and find true life. It's the new normal! If you and I do not live that way when we're with our spouses, let alone with everyone else, *we're restricted*, we're bound-up and robbed of Christ's ability within us . . . and left to something else—a performance.

Here's the question: Would you rather have Jesus' love for your spouse and for the people around you or your own? Would you prefer yours or your tagalong's?

Living in undivided devotion to Jesus ensures that they get His love—and that you do too.

You and I know that God is love (see 1 John 4:8 & 16). He doesn't just have love, He doesn't feel more loving one day and less the next, He doesn't offer love to those He finds particularly loveable—He *is* love. God is the *source* of love. Malcolm Smith writes, "I may tell you that I have a glass of water or a reservoir of water, but it is an entirely different category to say that I am water! To have water means that my possession of it is subject to change whether by increase or decrease, but to be water means I am never subject to change because it is what I am! He is the definition of love; love is the way He is." (*The Lost Secret of the New Covenant*, Harrison House, Inc., Tulsa, Oklahoma, 2002, p. 58.)

Genuine love comes from God. When you were brought into a favorable relationship with Him, you immediately began to know and discover real love. Relationship with God is the only relationship which can produce authentic love. That's why we become so devoted to Him—we do it for love! (And it's a high compliment when we do.)

No matter how good every other relationship is, it cannot produce love—it can only stimulate love. A weekend at a cabin by the lake with your wife thankfully elicits love and rekindles it, but it cannot *produce* love. Perhaps you've noticed that the longer you go without truly knowing God's love for you, the more dried up is your love for others. Given enough time without, you resort to dredging up some memory of love in order to act out what was once living within. But you know love is missing. Even though you are devoted to those around you, you're approaching empty, and only a return to God for who and what He is—love—will bring about the power of true love.

The wonder of that love is that it always extends to those around you, near and far. The longer you've been a Christian even with all your ups and downs, the more you've found within a resilient desire to know Him who is and produces love. That's not a selfish desire! Indulge it! God put it there because that's the normal way to live, and it's best for every relationship you've got.

Yet if you don't live for Love, for God and who and what He is, if you don't set up your day to know God and to be compelled by His love, sowing to the Spirit and indulging your deepest desire, you still have to be with people and you still have to behave. Without His love alive in you, your little inner well of life will begin to grow toxic and so will your relationships.

Here's an example of what might happen. We get with someone, our spouse or a roomful of people and we begin to think of all kinds of questions: "What would be the right thing for right now? What should happen here? How do I want to be perceived? What does she think of me? How should I approach them? What should be on my face? What about my body language? What should I say? As she looks at me, or as those in the room notice me, what do their faces say about me and what should I do about it?"

Our perceiver-expresser fills up with thoughts and feelings and a multitude of questions about what's needed or what to do. So instead of being aware of Jesus and instead of sowing to the Spirit right then, our awareness of everyone else gets bigger and Jesus disappears!

We can't feel Him, we can't hear Him, and we don't know what He's thinking because we're busy feeling, hearing, and thinking for Him! Not only are our thoughts consumed by earthly things, but we've given Him nothing to do. We lose the joy of being devoted to Jesus because we're working on our devotion to others. We're more devoted to the immediate relationship, the one we can see right in front of us and how we're doing in it, than we are devoted to Jesus and how He would do in it. In our thinking we're left all alone. That's toxic and it's not for us!

Religion persuades us to become preoccupied with the fruits and benefits of knowing God but not with the reality. So we commit too soon to doing whatever we perceive would be the best thing—the thing that would get us what we want, and we miss the One who lives within. And if we don't sow to the Spirit—looking and feeling and listening for Him—by default we sow to the flesh. You know what that means.

Satan schemes to turn us from the incredible enjoyment of the life we find in knowing Jesus to the life we believe we should have through proper employment of His principles. The life Jesus promised us is Himself, not the life of good relationships or the life of a happy home. He, who is our life, may be known and enjoyed at all times—whether happy and secure in relation to others or not, whether walking up the aisle at church or walking out the door at divorce court. Jesus is the way, the truth, and the life. He didn't say He would tell us the way to go, He didn't say He would tell us the truth, and He didn't say He would tell us about life so we could have a good one. He *is* the way! He *is* the truth! He *is* the life! (John 14:6). For Christians, true life is knowing God; everything else is a passing away picture of life. Speaking to the Father, Jesus said, "Now this is eternal life: that they may know you, the only true God, and Jesus Christ, whom you have sent" (John 17:3).

If I sow toward Him who lives in me and if I offer and devote myself to Him as I make my way through the day, turning my thoughts toward Him, I'll know Him, I'll hear Him, I'll feel Him and His love, and I'll be led in some manner toward those I meet. That's life! Christ formed in me (my tagalong) treats people and behaves toward others *through* me. He knows and loves them perfectly, He is concerned for them, knows their future, and has exactly what they need. What He is and what He has is way better than what I can muster up by the flesh, and it's all available to me! And it's available to them.

A terrific by-product, and perhaps the best part of it all, is that the burden and fear of how to say things just right, how to lead just right, and how to respond just right is lifted from me and, in my immediate submission to Jesus, I'm made a free man. I've placed my confidence and hope for relationships upon Him! It's amazing how much fear vanishes from my life when my chief effort is to know Jesus moment by moment. Not only when I'm praying or reading my Bible or worshiping Him at church—but throughout the day. To me, that's worship!

Paul wrote that he wanted the Corinthians to be free from concern, particularly that which had to do with pleasing their spouses (see 1 Corinthians 7:32-34). Did that freedom from concern about how to make their wives happy mean doom and gloom for their wives? Hardly! It meant that their marriages would not reflect those of the world around them, which were tragically awful, because they would benefit from the love, care, and ability of Christ in them. He would be at work and on display, the "profound mystery" for which God designed marriage in the first place (see Ephesians 5:21-33).

To assure them that he meant the best for them and their marriages, Paul wrote, "I am saying this for your own good, not to restrict you, but that you may live in a right way in undivided devotion to the Lord" (1 Corinthians 7:35). Marriage is a devotion divider, drawing the attention and devotion of the spouse away from the Lord and the issues of heaven and giving it to the spouse and the issues of earth and their demands. If and as we are drawn away from singular devotion, the production of love suffers. What happens to our relationships when that happens? We struggle to know what to do without the One who has no such difficulties. Relational frustration and eventual exhaustion is on the horizon. Devotional division will wear you out.

You've noticed that you have only so much devotion to give. If your devotion is like a pie, you have only so much to go around. Take a wife piece here (five tips on loving your wife), a daughter piece there (five techniques to grow a happy girl), and what's happening to your pie? It's diminishing. It's divided up. Not only that, but where your devotion is given to others, expectations and demands will be placed upon it and judgments will be made as to how effective it is. And off you'll go into the concerns and methods of this world, losing what your singular devotion to Christ had been giving you. You'll end up living again after the fashion of this world—by the flesh—and that's no way for you to live.

Singular devotion to Jesus, who is life, is the way to face your day—you're going to love it. However, you probably won't master your devotion immediately after reading this chapter; you're going to fumble a bit. The next time you feel the collision of devotional possibilities around people, you may be tempted to revert to former ways of relational navigation. Getting the response you want from people by figuring out what works best will continue for some time to be a powerful motivator. But going that route means you will lose the joy of knowing Jesus and it will cost you your freedom. You'll grow weary of the wrong way and prefer the true way. Besides, that old way of living doesn't work for you or anyone in Christ. When the divorce rate amongst Christians mirrors that of non-Christians, the evidence that worldly ways fail the church should be compelling.

It doesn't take a lot to notice how much like the world our relationships are these days. Out of understandable anxiety for the wreckage of relationships, we've been stuffing ourselves with how to be concerned for our spouses. Gleanings from well-meaning psychologists have indeed benefited many marriages, and I don't mean to suggest we shun them. However, the help received by couples is primarily at an elementary, relational level (a "here's how to get along with each other" level) rather than a Christian one. They took Manners 101 in nursery school ("Billy, it's not nice to paint on Mary's face . . ."), but now it's time for Manners 401. Couples don't absolutely have to have Jesus inside in order to have good relational skills, but no couple can grow in Christ without Him—and that's the goal of relationship. Employing relational skills, couples may feel better about each other and learn how to relate better (no small thing), but they don't know Jesus any better. They may be impressed with how good principles work, but they miss out on how Jesus in them actually works. It's unintentionally kept from them. What happens? Their hope remains in each other's ability to get enough tools and information in order to successfully have a relationship, as though that were the highest goal and the best place for their investment.

Let's say Bill and Mary go to a marriage enrichment seminar. They've worked long and tiring hours in order to get there, but their expectations for what they'll receive are high. In the first session they hear lots of funny stories about couples' differences in perception, talents and gifts, and desires and hopes. There's a lot to laugh about! In session two they're taught about their God-designed personalities, their love languages, how to understand what each other means *behind* their words, and about their disappointments. It's deep. Finally, in session three they're given the tools by which to have the caring and loving relationship they've always wanted. There might be time given to practice them and then, in the glow of vulnerability, they head home to put it all into practice. What a weekend. Only it's not long before the weekend is long gone.

In the end what Bill and Mary learned is what to do out of concern for each other. Seems good but that's exactly how the natural life of this world works–here's what you should care about and here's what you should do. And that's exactly what Paul warns us not to do. Our couple has been loaded up with concern for each other and the how-to-meet-that-concern produced by that knowledge.

It won't be long before our glowing couple will be reduced to gloom. Mary will notice that Bill has slacked off in his commitment to cherish her; it will bother her. And, in view of his commitment failure, hers will be affected . . . and she'll know it. Gloom. Bill will slowly notice a withdrawn and gloomy Mary, and ask the obvious question: "Honey, what's wrong?"

Mary will either stuff her feelings and impressions with a brilliant and convincing, "Oh, nothing." Or she'll say, "I don't feel loved by you . . . I can't believe you've gone back so soon to the way you were before the retreat. . . ." And now, gloomy Bill.

It may not be precisely this way, but this is the typical scenario. Over the span of a weekend, our now gloomy couple was educated as to "how things are" and "how things work" and yet, graduation resulted in a failure of love. By relying upon their educated concern for each other love is turned aside.

And what's left are two unhappy and unwitting Pharisees who, after finding each other wanting, sleep in the same bed—near but far away. Christian growth must not become all about working smarter and better with each other rather than finding Christ within. Transformation must not become a self-improvement makeover, rather than a life found within and released without. Working as hard as they can, Bill and Mary may wind up with a form of godly relationship (they get along well enough), but they will have been robbed of the power a godly relationship provides.

It's likely that sometime in the future, one or both will break down and admit their inadequacy, calling on the Lord. And you know what happens then—love makes a come back. Love from God always means love for others. What they've actually been looking for is the *result* of God's work in them. And they can have that any time.

When Paul faced an antagonistic crowd of pagans who had never before heard the Gospel, he didn't rely upon his upbringing, nor his training under Gamaliel, nor his own savvy way of reaching particularly nasty Corinthian pagans. He writes,

> When I came to you, brothers, I did not come with eloquence or superior wisdom as I proclaimed to you the testimony about God. *For I resolved to know nothing while I was with you except Jesus Christ and him crucified.* (1 Corinthians 2:1-2, italics mine)

I don't know about you, but before I faced a dangerous crowd of unbelievers, I would be tempted to prepare a lot more than that! I'd invest in a demographic study, find out where certain parts of town were, plan to provide plenty of food and refreshments, make sure my presentation was tight, enlist armies of prayer warriors, and map-out the quickest route out of town— just in case! But not Paul. He relied upon knowing Christ right in front of the pagan crowd, his best and highest course for action. How did his body respond and what was the result?

> I came to you in weakness and fear, and with much trembling. My message and my preaching were not with wise and persuasive words, but with a demonstration of the Spirit's power, *so that your faith might not rest on men's wisdom, but on God's power.* (1 Corinthians 2:1-5, italics mine)

Because he wasn't employing his own techniques, but instead was relying upon the mystery of Christ in Him, his body felt alarm—but look what happened! The Holy Spirit demonstrated Himself! What else was needed? It's common that many Christians today suffer from a lack of certainty that they have indeed been saved, perhaps because they were aggressively talked into it or because the appeal was so grand and perfect, but it's not likely that Paul's hearers did. *They knew* because God's power made sure they did. What a relief.

This is one of the ways by which we live "in the new way of the Spirit," and not after the manner by which those under the former covenant lived (see Romans 7:6). Unlike them, we live by faith in God's ability from within us as well as around us, and that distinction must be made so it can be lived out. We should expect Him to work within us—it's His gift and our thrill!

Since Paul expected so much from Christ within, he was able and encouraged to make himself a slave to all men; this is how and why he could! (See 1 Corinthians 9:19.) With God inside, what could happen to Paul outside of God's influence? And think of the daily anticipation—every encounter an adventure; each appointment a wonder! What will God do next? The will and purposes of God will be known by you because He will be at work within! And that's the Christian life.

A couple of years ago, I was speaking to a group of wonderful Christian punker-types. Perhaps you've seen some: bodies pierced, hair done up in outrageous angles and colors, and a mishmash of clothing borrowed from circus performers. They tell me that most people avoid them, which is pretty much what they want. By no plan of our own, we've hit it off. Think of it: my hair, clothing, look, and manner are conservative in most every way, the exact opposite of what they would normally accept, and they are the same for me. And yet, we love! Why? Christ in us.

At the end of one night's seminar, a young woman asked if I might like to have a cigarette with her—a way to invite me to talk. As we sat down, I thought, "Holy Spirit, I am glad you're in me, ready to do so much. I love you and offer myself to you for whatever you would like . . ." As she talked about fairly light things, I listened with one ear and gave the other to the Spirit. A few minutes passed when I heard Him say, "Ask her how long she has been a cutter." Now, because that's a very difficult thing to approach, I again offered myself to Him and heard the same thing. While my fleshly mind put up a bit of a struggle on the surface of my awareness, I was still enjoying a deeper contentment in Him, so I asked the question. I didn't dress it up or make it palatable with a "thus sayeth God," or a "I sort of feel maybe like God wants to tell you He loves you," but calmly asked what I knew to ask.

You know what happened? Her mouth agape, she peeled back first one pant leg, then the other, and then moved to her sleeves, all the while wondering how I could know such a dark and secretive thing . . . and how I could know without even a hint of condemnation or shame toward her. Scores of uniformly neat razor scars laid bare, she had little to hide before Mr. Conservative. As her face grew flush and her cheeks wet with tears, she poured out her many tormenting fears, as well as the misshapen remains of genuine hope and love for God. Think how gloomy little miss punker had been. She wanted God more than anything, but didn't think the desire was mutual. Think what it must have felt like to find out it *was*.

She was rescued through me that night, and her faith rested with Him and not with me. But I got the thrill of the thing. Look for Him, devote yourself to finding Him and feeling Him, experiencing the delight of His presence right in front of others. You'll be free from the tyranny of the urgent because you'll be knowing the grace of the One who is in no hurry.

Chapter Ten

Friendship With Our Friend

A man of many companions may come to ruin,
but there is a friend who sticks closer than a
brother. (Proverbs 18:24)

Doug is his name. There are at least one hundred and thirty-two people who believe they are best friends with Doug. By now there are more. Doug is not only genuine, fun, unassuming, brilliant, and sincere, he is there *for me* in a way which sometimes makes me uncomfortable. I might be struggling to keep myself together during some trying day or circumstance, and Doug will just happen to call. Hearing the stress in my voice after I've told him how bad I've got it, he'll ask, "So, how are you?" Now, what I really want is sympathy ("Man! I can't believe what's going on around you!") or a collaborative offer ("I'm comin' over there and we'll take care of this together!"). What I think would be perfect is that he would just run over and give me a pep talk along with an adrenaline injection. What a friend—my personal coach and pusher.

But no. Not Doug.

He'll ask, "Ralph, what are you feeling? Why does this bother you? What do you think God is doing right now?" Isn't that awful? Who has *time* for that! What I want is renewed strength and clarity so I can get the job done, not an uncomfortable probe!

I might respond, "Look! I'm feeling just a little mad because things are in chaos and, happily seated on His throne, God is not budging! I'm trying to serve Him and He's not helping."

And Doug might say, "Yeah. I can sure understand that. It must feel exactly like that. But what are you trying to do that He won't?"

And there it is. A harpoon where I needed it—right to my flesh.

I'm suddenly aware that I've been chasing a goal like Ahab chased Moby Dick. Slaving away and pushing the crew of my own *Pequod* in order to get close enough to plunge the harpoon directly into the side of my project and thereby conquering it, I've become entangled by my efforts to slay the beast. Moby Dick has me and, gasping for air, I've been taking an awful dunking ever since.

My friend cut me loose. I had been working way too hard at something God was not doing, but I couldn't let go of it. Whenever that happens, the real Ralph disappears in favor of an actor who can get the job done—Ralph for Ahab. His crew may fear him, but the ship does move. Whatever it takes, get the job done, right? ("Hello" to Brute and Nike flesh!) Only I'm lost in the process. Even if everyone is serving the agreed upon purpose (*Get Moby!*), God has little to do with it—*everyone's lost.*

It's right then I need a friend. Doug likes me and likes to be with me, but he insists upon authenticity when we're together. If he thinks Ralph has become a flesh bag (*"Thar she blows!"*), he is alarmed enough to help me. That way, we can get the most out of our friendship. Even though it sometimes feels like he is against me, he is all about saving me all the time and I love him for it. His harpoons are directed at my flesh because he knows and loves my heart.

My friend is a lot like Jesus.

In our day it's common to speak of believers as warriors and servants and disciples and, in its place, that's well and good. We *are*. Many a believer has been rightly motivated to action by such scriptural reference.

However, consider that (in our desire to inspire) we may have overemphasized our warrior and servant status while neglecting our desirability as *friend of God*.

How often do we think of ourselves as being sought after by God for much more than to give us our orders for the front lines? Perhaps a semi-stern talking to? A calling on the carpet? A little finger-wagging in the face? Or perhaps for an opportunity for us to fess up and repent?

While the letter the Holy Spirit wrote through Paul speaks of an outlandish, even eccentric love and grace "lavished upon us" already (Ephesians 1:4-8), many of us feel as though our love-crazed Groom is now hesitant concerning our impending nuptials. Like He doesn't have that look in His eye He once did when gazing upon us. It's not so, but it may be what we think.

What if God likes to be around you because He believes you're His friend? Is it possible that while we make a big deal of being servants of the King, the Emperor Himself has something additional in view?

> "I no longer call you servants, because a servant does not know his master's business. Instead, I have called you *friends*, for everything that I learned from my Father I have made known to you." (John 15:15, italics mine)

In this chapter I simply mean to keep you to what His opinion of you is and, perhaps, stretch it out a bit. Approaching Him upon the basis of what He has already made of you, drawing near to Him, speaking to Him, or listening to Him in faith about what He thinks of you is the way to invigorated life and awe. It is also the way to recognize just how much He seeks you out . . . to spend a few moments, to share a secret, to drive out a fear, to remove an anxiety by telling you the truth, to provide joy, love, and peace. He's really good at being your friend because He has actually made you His friend.

Friends like each other. Friends share secrets. Friends laugh together. Friends make plans together. Friends rely upon each other through thick and thin and are intimately involved in each other's lives. They are *for* each other.

Could you accept that God might approach you today for no other reason than that He likes you? Or because the way you encourage and make people laugh makes Him happy? Or that how you notice people and go out of your way to sincerely compliment them pleases Him! He likes being with you to watch! Or maybe your style of clothing, hair length or color, or even the way you zip around the corners in your car brings a smile to His face. Could He have made you so well and so right

wow

that He likes to be with you in a way that is obvious and delightful?

Singer Wayne Watson has it right:

I had this dream and You were in it
There was this party and You were there
Simple evening with just a few close friends
People were pressing for Your attention
You were patient, everybody could see
But all the time You were lookin' round the room for me
But hey, after all, it's my dream

Chorus
I wanna be the kind of friend that Jesus would call
You know if He had a telephone
At the end of the day
Just to talk about nothin', nothin'
Yeah, I wanna be the kind of friend He'd wanna be around
You know without a word, without a sound
Wouldn't that be somethin', somethin', yeah

Is that so hard to imagine
The Lord Jesus as a friend like that
Spending time in the pleasure of your company
True companion like no other
Oh, you never had a friend like this
If you're havin' a little trouble believing
Come on, put yourself in my dream

(Chorus)

Wouldn't that be somethin', somethin', yeah

You can figure that in any of the many ways God describes Himself, He's the best at it. He is loving—there's no one more so. He is merciful—His compassionate feelings run deepest, and His helpfulness is unrelenting. He is understanding—it gets no better than Him. He is faithful—without flaw! He is your friend—is there a better one? Nope.

I think, that in all of our attempts at service and discipleship, the best ingredient is friendship with our Friend. Without it, service and discipleship become qualities necessary for employment with God, dry and measurable, always under scrutiny by the Big Boss. Did you punch your time card today? Were you on time? Did you have a pleasing attitude? Did you whistle while you worked?

Have you ever gotten tired of serving, serving, serving? What ended your fatigue? Wasn't it when you stopped and got off the job? Doesn't that tell you that there's something missing in your service? There is! It's friendship with God. While ultimately He is the Big Boss in the Big Office, He doesn't confine Himself to *proper relationships* commensurate to His status, shunning interaction with the lower subjects of His corporation. He's with you! Right there on the job, sharing in your labor, delighting in your style, making much of Himself by pointing at you in front of the angels. He enjoys you!

I don't mean to demean service to God—it's just that many of us have been kept from the delight and honor of it because we're so concerned with how we're doing it and that we have to! Nowadays we commonly measure ourselves by the amount and quality of our service but rarely by the enjoyment of our friendship with our Friend.

One of the most startling things I used to tell the people in ministry with me, be it Children's, Youth, Music, Women's, etc., was that they didn't have to do it. "Cathe, there's no one collecting your time card at the end of this week, you know." If service to God has become a grinding drudgery, the antidote is not more service or less—it's a renewal of friendship with God. Discovering that we can enjoy His friendship *on the job* is what keeps us well *in the job*. When serving becomes more important than friendship with Him, the life and value go out of it, and you know what a power outage that is.

Serving God is a high calling—friendship with God is not the cost but the fuel. Yet if we can be sold on the idea that service is the highest compliment to God and not love reciprocated and friendship enjoyed, then Satan can soon weary us and prevent the full stature of who and what we are from emerging. Something of the glory of God gets hidden.

But what if we give ourselves to enjoying God and His friendship with us? Will we get much out of it? Will we still serve Him? Will it help us on the job and make a car payment? Yes! Sort of. Friends love each other and love works. More specifically, love invigorates and *compels* us; it motivates us and carries us into the day in order to see where it might rush out, as Paul wrote in 2 Corinthians 5:14. It's relatively effortless, like a perfect stream moving through you. And couldn't you use a little bit of that on the job? How about around home? Or in your relationships?

Let me ask you this: if you spent a day dwelling upon and enjoying the love God has for you, would you expect to receive an infusion of power, some real *"Ooomph"* for your day? Would you expect to be supplied, pushed, and driven by it and think that it would be the best thing for your day?

Many of us treat the love of God as though it were a rarely needed winter coat. "Sure glad I've got that jacket in the closet. I know it's there for when I *really* need it." We're even working hard to *not* need it, cramming ourselves with "how to love" sermons and books, and seminaring ourselves nearly to death on ways to act and approach people as though love were truly compelling us. Since it's not the style of the Holy Spirit to ever condemn one of His own, I don't mean to either. Yet isn't it strange we go on our way, day after day, missing love and calling it *normal*? No wonder the practicality of learning and speaking the love language of those around you is so appealing—we've a vacuum to fill.

And you're no dummy. You're not avoiding God's love as though some sort of masochistic tendency were keeping you from deepest satisfaction. Nope. This whole thing has been and continues to be the effort of the enemy.

I believe that we've been lured away from love and friendship with God because we've become dependent upon finding *another kind* of compelling, one which seems promising and possible for our day. We make or buy beverages to get us going *(Hooray for Starbucks with an extra shot!)*, we go to seminars to get us going, we read books and go to church to get us going, we go to school and marry spouses to get us going. We even take vacations to get us going. Nothing is wrong with these things (except maybe a little addiction to caffeine) unless they keep us from discovering the power we get from God. And frequently they do. It's rare that we grasp how the terrific, yet simple, ingredients of love and friendship with God provide genuine get-up-and-go for our every day. If we did, we would make knowing His love the indispensable priority it ought to be.

God is love (see 1 John 4:7-12). God doesn't *have* love, God's love doesn't ebb and flow, rise and fall, motivated by the subject—God *is* love. He looks always to satisfy His love in those who receive it. And when you and I know it, believe it, and are convinced by it, His love comes together . . . and usually goes somewhere and does something. It compels. That's why He invites us so much to love . . . I think it is highest priority with Him for you and me.

When we fail and break down, it's not a failure of service or of proper discipleship, it's a failure of love. And God's love is at all times lavished upon us because of His grace to us in Christ. Knowing what He thinks of you, knowing why He approaches you in the manner He does (as a friend!) is all because of grace! Approaching Him as a friend will affect your life. In love you'll look and act like a servant and disciple of Christ. With appreciated grace in evidence—*you'll look great*.

Augustine wrote, "If you but love God you may do as you incline." He was serious! A person in love with God will be inclined to do whatever it takes to please Him. That's what love does to us. And that's why Jesus and Paul summed up the law with one command, "*Love God*."

Here's what I suggest: lay aside your worker-bee identity, your servant-oriented, warrior-in-the-Kingdom distinctiveness, and be willing to accept a real friendship with God. Ask Him about it! You won't lose anything worth keeping, and you'll get God in a particularly satisfying way. You'll love it and He will too.

Chapter Eleven

The Eyes Have It

So from now on we regard no one from a worldly point of view. Though we once regarded Christ in this way, we do so no longer.
(2 Corinthians 5:16)

Over the last couple of years my maturing eyesight has caused my Bible to creep further and further from my face making reading it a wrestling match for focus. I've been feeling like an SLR camera, searching for the optimal range, my hands holding my reading near, then further away, still further away, only to exceed the perfect distance, requiring a reversal of the whole process. Since I've never had any problems with my eyesight I was very frustrated and I remember thinking, "What's the deal? Why is it so difficult to focus? Is there something wrong with my eyes? I've got to be able to focus!"

Where hanging reading glasses on my face solved *that* focus problem, it brought to light a more serious issue of focus in my life: my eyes don't tell me the truth.

There are times when I'm confident I would have sided with the ten Hebrews sent on reconnaissance into the Land of Promise, loudly arguing with those two imbeciles in denial, Joshua and Caleb. "Did you happen to *look around*, Joshua? Did you happen to notice everyone in Goshen is a big brother to Shaquille O'Neal? I'd rather get into the ring with one of those WWF monsters than wander into *their* territory! Think of our families! Think of our future! Do you suppose this to be a wise move? You may be a big man on campus around here, Caleb, but over there you're Mini Me!"

Only two out of twelve had it right, but those two weren't seeing what the ten were seeing. While surely noticing the men looked like gigantic Dennis Rodmans, Joshua and Caleb were kept sane by the truth when confronted with what they saw. The truth was the greater influence. "Be strong and courageous, because you will lead these people to inherit the land I swore to their forefathers to give them" (Joshua 1:6). The ten who reported and wanted to live according to what they saw went temporarily insane, forgetting who they were and who was with them. Sometimes I'm among their number.

God had long promised a land loaded with good stuff for His people, and *that* they could understand, *that* they could imagine. No doubt they expected easy livin' at Resort du Promised Land.

One problem: the neighbors.

Nobody on the block was about to respect who the Israelites were; not the Canaanites, Hittites, Amorites, Perizzites, Hivites, or Jebusites. They were wicked people, rivaling any of today's worst. If the children of God were to live next door to Ozzy Ozbourne and company, one of two things would happen: they would cling fiercely to the truth in the midst of severe opposition to it (". . . do not turn from it to the right or to the left, that you may be successful wherever you go . . ."), or they would let their eyes do the talking, conforming their lives to what they reported.

Well, you know how it went—*the eyes had 'em.* For much of the time, they lived *out of focus*, and I'm concerned we do too. What happened to our ancestors happens to us—we forget who we are (and who people are) when our consistent gaze leaves the truth which defines us and which provides focus for our lives, and we drift toward the appeal of outward appearances, the temporal facades of the world around us. After all, that show is always on. So our eyes fake us out. When they do, our approach to life goes with them—we can't help it.

Here's an example. Let's say you've heard some particularly distressing things about a local church you used to attend. You've been told by more than a few that there is rampant hypocrisy amongst the members, as well as lying, cheating, smoking, doping, stealing, drinking, immoral sex, and the like. They're looking ugly. For all the wrong reasons, they've even made the newspaper. Further, no one there seems of a mind to stop what they're doing—repentance isn't on anyone's agenda.

Monday morning brings a phone call from one of that church's elders with a unique request. He wonders if you've heard what's been going on at his church, and, after you tell him that you have, he gives even more grimy details. He then asks, "On behalf of the elders I wonder if you would write a letter to our congregation addressing our situation, which I will read to the church this coming Sunday. Whatever you write, they will hear. Will you?"

Feeling the weight of the moment, you nevertheless respond, "Yes, I will."

So what's going to be in your letter? What do you have to say to those awful behaving, unrepentant, backslidden believers? You'll have their attention—what do you give them?

Essentially, that's what happened to the apostle Paul, who, by the grace of God, penned his first letter to the Christians at Corinth. Like you, he had heard all about the ugly and awful behavior of the church and wrote a letter for them all to hear. He would have their attention—what would he write?

> Paul, called as an apostle of Jesus Christ by the will of God, and Sosthenes our brother, to the church of God which is at Corinth, to those who have been sanctified in Christ Jesus, saints by calling, with all who in every place call upon the name of our Lord Jesus Christ, their Lord and ours: Grace to you and peace from God our Father and the Lord Jesus Christ. I thank my God always concerning you, for the grace of God which was given you in Christ Jesus, that in everything you were enriched in Him, in all speech and all knowledge, even as the testimony concerning Christ was confirmed in you, so that you are not lacking in any gift, awaiting eagerly the revelation of our Lord Jesus Christ, who will also confirm you to the end, blameless in the day of our Lord Jesus Christ. God is faithful, through whom you were called into fellowship with His Son, Jesus Christ our Lord. (1 Corinthians 1:1-9 NAS)

What's wrong with Paul? "*Grace* to you and *peace* from God our Father and the Lord Jesus Christ"? Is he kidding? Why would he write a thing like that? Isn't that an awfully big assumption? They were "enriched in Him, in all speech and all knowledge," and "not lacking in any gift"? And these misbehaving believers would be kept *"blameless"* until the end! Paul, how can that be? Can't you see what they're doing!

The Corinthian Christians were plenty guilty of plenty of things and he addresses them like that? Since we're able to read ahead in Paul's letter, we know that they were looking and acting a lot like the pagans of Corinth because Paul spent the majority of his letter correcting them. They were guilty of drunkenness (1 Corinthians 11:21), sexual immorality and fornication (5:1f), of taking each other to court and cheating (6:1-8), of divorce (7), of being a divided church (1:10f), of stubbornly remaining infantile in their faith and worldly in their living (3:1-3), of arrogance (4:18) and more. Don't you think Paul should have lowered the heavenly boom on them and knocked a little sense into them? Did you in your letter? Most of us would.

Why would Paul, who knew all about what they were doing and who knew more than most anyone what an affront sin is to God, first speak to them in such a way? Why not first give them a good righteous whack across their unrepentant backsides?

Here's why: When Paul thought of the Corinthians, he thought of them as they had *become*, not as they behaved. He lived by faith, not by sight (2 Corinthians 5:7), and that framed every view for Paul.

He knew that if they were acting in ways contrary to whom they had become, it was because they had forgotten whom they had become! Paul's first duty was not to the correction of their behavior ("Stop that, you cruddy Corinthians!") but to the awakening of their faith in God who had made them sons!

Paul approached the Corinthians not with a behavior-curtailing whack but with an attempt to draw them back to worship. They needed revival more than they needed restraint! The Corinthian Christians looked ugly and did ugly things not because they were in fact ugly but because they had become ugly in their thinking. They had forgotten the majesty of God's mercy to them in Christ (forgiven!) and the incredible change He had made for them (new creation!) and their behavior made it

However, the camera has no close-up focus of its own; in order to get an accurate close-up, I have to move my entire body nearer to or further away in order to get in the right position for the best view and picture. More than once I have returned from a mountain trip, hooked up the camera to our television for the family to enjoy the pictures I've taken, only to groan when discovering what must have been a stunning wildflower blurred by improper focus. It ruins everything, there is no joy, and there is no way to rectify it. It's not long before the memory of that flower in all its splendor has faded, soon to be forgotten.

I think that happens to us when somewhere along the line, for some reason, we stop moving our lives in an effort to get the best, most accurate, and revealing focus. Oh, we may continue to act well, to ask for God's blessings, and to do pretty good things, but *who we are* loses its power because we can't *see* anymore. But we *must*.

Think of the apostle Paul, who, having discovered who he had become in Christ, spent years amongst the unloved, unlovely believers of his day convincing them they had been made *far better* through Christ (Colossians 1:28-29). What a struggle that must have been! Those chosen of God, bought and remade by Him, no doubt wrestled with the ever-offered lie that they were still the ungainly misfits of that day; they might as well fit in as best they could. Paul knew better and worked to see they did too.

> Once you were alienated from God and were enemies in your minds because of your evil behavior. But now he has reconciled you by Christ's physical body through death to present you holy in his sight, without blemish *and free from accusation—if you continue in your faith*, established and firm, *not moved* from the hope held out in the gospel. This is the gospel that you heard and that has been proclaimed to every creature under heaven, and of which I, Paul, have become a servant. (Colossians 1:21-23, italics mine)

What a great truth to tell the Colossians. But maybe you know how it goes when, like them, you lose focus and forget what God's opinion of you and of others is because you see only what your eyes tell you—your faith fails and you are no longer *"free from accusation."* When you see a believer (or yourself) do something or behave in a way contrary to who they are in Christ, you may forget who they are in Christ—and move away from the Gospel, no longer continuing in your faith. Every little hurtful or evil thought about you (I'm terrible!) and about others (they're terrible!) will grab and hold your attention, drawing you away from the eternal truth of who people are in Christ. And your efforts with people will follow along with those accusations because you will have been moved from the Gospel.

But you don't have to move. Try this: the next time you see a Christian, look beyond what you can see. Look to what God says is true of them (since He made it happen!) and tell them about it right then and there. "Hello, my friend. Isn't it amazing that as you stand there you are a holy son of God, a blameless, radiant, and righteous friend of His? While you're stuck in the chaos and turmoil of this world, you are not at all *of* it and it is not worthy of you. I know who you are, and I'm thrilled with God because of you."

Watch their face, because their faith and focus will be revealed as you accurately describe them. Two things will likely happen: Either they will smile and happily embrace what you've shared ("Oh, thank you for reminding me!"), or they will frown and disagree ("Well, I'm not so sure about *that*."). Either way, you're turning their thoughts to what God thinks of them and that's worth a little fuss! If your Christian friend has been in anything like the same fight for faith you've been in, you may safely assume your approach to them is rescuing them. They really do not fit with the ten spies whose eyes alone had them, but with Joshua and Caleb who were focused by faith! So gently press on because you know that for everyone the Gospel "is the power of God . . ." (Romans 1:16). What God thinks of them has power when it is believed; they will feel it, and their renewed focus will give them a mini revival.

And do you wonder about spiritual warfare? This is its true launching point! Think of the harm you've done to the devil and his plans. You haven't simply given a bewildered believer a weapon or two, (something to *claim* and something to *proclaim*) and told him how to use them, you've wakened him to who is with him and who he is–what a triumph that is! He doesn't just know how to work a weapon and swing a sword, he knows his fit with God–what can prevail against him? Nothing!

I imagine Joshua and Caleb could have outfitted the deluded ten with as many weapons as they wanted and still they would have refused to enter God's promise. What they saw had flooded-out what they at one time knew–God was with them and they were His chosen! But the Land of Promise became the land of delusion because their eyes had them. But not yours.

Since we've not commonly thought about life according to the invisible realm, I want to make some suggestions. For the most part, we've become accustomed to a pattern of living which seems to work and "get us by" in our relationships with people. In other words, our eyes control us—we see something and act in keeping with what we see. It's a habit. If you're going to break out of the pattern and approach people as they truly are, you'll need to intentionally do something to see through the facade which confronts you and to prefer what's invisible—that's what you're all about.

Consider turning away from nightly television viewing which inoculates us against the invisible by giving us a big dose of the visible. Read the New Testament which draws us into the real world as it really is for us. Resist the urge to act according to what seems normal or usual in a common situation by pausing and sowing to the Spirit. Living by faith in God's opinion is an exhilarating exercise offered all day long.

You may want to think of some situations in which you can prefer the invisible by rejecting the visible. Perhaps you've treated someone in a way that "seems right" and "gets it done," but which now seems anything but sufficient. How might it be different? How might you approach those you know are Christians but, when you're around them, you've never thought of them as being holy, blameless, and righteous sons of God? There they are—right in front of you! What might be different the next time?

Grow accustomed to relying upon the unseen when you're with people. It's likely they won't see what you do, but they can—they need to. You might even pray as Elijah did so long ago, when, surrounded by an enemy sent to capture him, he prayed for his unseeing servant.

"Oh, my lord, what shall we do?" the servant asked. "Don't be afraid," the prophet answered. "Those who are with us are more than those who are with them." And Elisha prayed, "O LORD, open his eyes so he may see." Then the LORD opened the servant's eyes, and he looked and saw the hills full of horses and chariots of fire all around Elisha. (2 Kings 6:15-17)

Chapter Twelve
Aliens Have Landed

Dear friends, I urge you, as aliens and strangers in the world, to abstain from sinful desires, which war against your soul. (1 Peter 2:11)

"Oh, I *hate* school! Why do I have to go, Daddy?" Having recently returned from an idyllic family time in Jackson Hole, Wyoming, Ellen was venting her frustration about starting the school year . . . venting like a hurricane.

Emma, ever the opportunist, offered her own timely impression of a cyclone. "Yeah! I hate school, too! It stinks! And I didn't get the teacher I wanted either. I don't want to go!"

And the two storms merged into a gale-force "*Waaaaaaaaaaaaaaaaaaaaah!*"

It was category 5 in my house. In the face of ferocious complaining, I considered fleeing to higher ground—every man for himself. Or, maybe I should just raise my voice, show 'em what a real hurricane is like, and shut down their miserable whining—snuff out the storm and restore order to my home. Yeah, that's it . . . that'll work.

But it misses what's really going on. God was at work in my daughters and I was a tad slow in recognizing it.

Each day that Ellen and Emma navigate the masses of moms and dadsshepherding their little ones to their classrooms, they enter a realm which not only fails to recognize them but which instead assaults them. No matter how student-friendly the classroom, no matter the good rules given for respectful relationships, no matter the kindness of the smiling teachers, my daughters spend five days a week as aliens in a foreign world. How torturous! How frustrating!

Having been born from above, Ellen and Emma are as alien to this world as Jesus (John 17:16), and it shouldn't surprise me when they feel it. *They must!* And they do—thank God. What if they didn't?

Much has been written about how to foster and secure the good behavior of our children, as well as how to educate them so they will be successful in life. Today there are countless volumes of material aimed at educating parents about the requirements and costs of properly raising their children. It will take devotion, time, commitment, vigilance, fortitude, and a clear plan to raise obedient children.

But is that really the goal? And what if I occasionally get lazy? What if I blow up or break down now and then? Or what if my kids don't respond properly to my maxims—just how far do I go toward insisting they acquiesce? There may be times I can't tell the difference between them being rebellious and them having warranted frustration with me. Is there ever a time I let up on them and allow them to do what they want—would that be so bad? And if I have toe-the-line kids, whose behavior is beyond reproach from school to market to church but have no true heartfelt intimacy and fellowship with them, that's not really success. What will I have raised—well-behaved women who know how to behave and live with a Pharisee? My girls could grow up to be women who relate to God on a similar basis.

Here's my confession: I regularly fail to do everything right with my kids. Fortunately, while I don't mean to make light of failure, doing everything right is not my goal. I want them to know God—that's my goal. More than to do well and be successful, more than to fit in and be liked and well-behaved—I want them to know God; where He is, what He thinks, how He feels, and what He is doing. I want that. And since my children have been made into His daughters, I must agree and begin with what He thinks of them and approach them from there. *God tells me who my children are.* I believe Him and move from that point. Anything else gets in the way.

The primary struggle my children have is the same as mine—to believe what God thinks about them and to live from it.

The biggest difference is one of experience. I have years of navigating this world's identity offerings (including Sports Star,

Genius, Don Juan, and Pastor Extraordinaire) and found that each of those identities required too much and returned too little. Even after the shocking joy of discovering who I am in Christ, still the lure to morph into something more valued in the eyes of this world proved at times irresistible. My glance down the memory lane of fifty years reminds me of how thrilled I was at the intersection of God's revelation, but that hasn't meant a straight road following. I've looked all over the place for an identity I liked and could work best to my advantage. The identity supermarket of this world has filled up my cart, and it takes serious effort to throw out the false selves collected there. They're not me! But they're so convenient . . . they've come in handy before.

My daughters aren't so loaded up though. Ellen and Emma will have to walk the same worldly aisles as Sarah and I, and screaming, "Choose me!" from the shelves, will be virtually all the desirable identities available to everyone. If they don't have as their foundation who they already are, the odds are great they'll begin filling their carts. I did.

This is not to say that all we want to give them is a healthy self-esteem. Often the response of the church to the perceived fragileness of its children is to strongly advocate we do our best to make our kids feel accepted, loved, and properly led at home so they'll do well when they leave it. We've majored on boundaries, discipline, quality time, follow-through, and on the united front presented by mom and dad. None of these is by itself wrong, but all these together fall way short. They are prescriptions for life without answering the question, "Who am I in this life?"

In my formative years I failed to ask that question because I didn't need to know! All I was concerned about was getting and avoiding what I wanted and didn't want, which could be secured by putting together the proper list of methods and techniques sure to get me there. I was entranced! And who wouldn't be? I was of this world and I was intent on playing its game. I didn't approach life as though I already was someone, but as though I was on the way to *become* someone.

All the world seemed to tell me "this is the way to the life you want and the 'you' you want to be," which meant, in essence, I could do well and be worshiped. What a trick! Be a sports star and everyone will rank you at the top. Be a genius and everybody will marvel at your intellect. Become a Don Juan and everyone will know you're "it." Be a Pastor Extraordinaire and the gathering crowd will knowingly nod as you pass by. You got it . . . you made it. Only what you *got* covered over who you *are*, and your arrival obscured your beginning.

If learning how to live and applying yourself to that is ranked ahead of *who you are* in this life *already* (if you're eight or eighty), your days will be spent loading your cart at the identity market. You'll labor to construct a "you" which will work in any scenario, a facade which you can slip on as the need arises. What will haunt you is that your persona—your "you"—will fail and be found out. With worldly success and admiration your goal, fear will become your silent motivator.

This early pattern for life is what usually brings confused and frustrated Christians to the later goal of weaning themselves off of this world. By then it takes Herculean effort. Season after season, year after year, we've given ourselves to what makes life work best, and when God works to mature us in keeping with what He knows is true, we feel He is against us. "Why isn't my life working?" comes the question. Because we've been sold a way of life without the definition of life.

Our Christian children are aliens. If they don't know it, or if we teach them only techniques to be successful in this life, as though that were Christian, we've set them up for frustration. When I see a trained monkey wearing children's clothing and playing with children's toys, I think it's cute but I'm not confused. It's not natural! I don't leap and exclaim, "Wow! The monkey has become a kid! What shall we name him?" In the same way, as I train my children to function in this world, what must remain clear, to them and to me, is that they are not of this world! They're from another. If they don't know it, their deluded attempt to fit with this world will make monkeys out of them.

Our Christian children are lights in this world, holy and blameless sons of God in whom lives the Holy Spirit Himself. They're not on a long and winding path at the end of which (if successfully negotiated) they will arrive—they've *arrived already*.

Do you see them? Not if you're looking at them only with the eyes in your head and not the eyes in your heart. Paul prayed,

> I keep asking that the God of our Lord Jesus Christ, the glorious Father, may give you the Spirit of wisdom and revelation, so that you may know him better. I pray also that the eyes of your heart may be enlightened in order that you may know the hope to which he has called you, the riches of his glorious inheritance in the saints, and his incomparably great power for us who believe. (Ephesians 1:17-19)

The "glorious inheritance" in our children right now is more fantastic than anything else in this world. Just because it isn't easy to see is no reason to turn away and quit looking! The need for revelation is another of God's invitations to know and be satisfied by Him and to be transformed into His likeness. When the Spirit reveals to me what He thinks about Ellen and Emma, I believe Him and approach them from there. In other words, I look and feel a whole lot like Jesus because I'm living by faith! And any opportunity to do that is wonderfully satisfying—it fits who I am.

If we don't know what He has in mind when we look at our children, then we'll invent something instead and it will never match up. We don't "live by faith and not by sight" *only* in God's promises, but also in what God says He has done for people and made them to be. We see all of life according to His opinion.

Who and what my daughters have become is fantastic, yet if they don't know it, the odds are great that they'll get lost in this world, believing they are merely human, though favored by God. I cannot tell you how many times I have heard a Christian say, "Well, I'm only human" regarding some failure or frustration, an excuse for behaving in a poor manner. Having been thoroughly educated in this world's pattern, they think of themselves as human first—*merely man*—and son of God second, flesh rather than spirit. However acceptable this thinking has become, it is not accurate and should be corrected.

Since there was "jealousy and strife" amongst the Corinthian believers, Paul, knowing exactly who they were in Christ, rebuked them for behaving so "fleshly," and for "walking like mere men" (1 Corinthians 3:1-3). In other words, we might say today, "Hey! You're not like that, you're not just human anymore, so knock that stuff off. You've been changed into something far greater."

Every believer, regardless of age, is as foreign to this world as was Jesus. Christians don't even have to open their mouths and they're targeted for spiritual Terrorism—they're marked in Christ (Ephesians 1:13) and have become violators of the satanic worldly order. Surely that explains much of the conflict we have in it; we are being identified as permanent strangers to the system (John 15:19). The extent of our attempts to conform ourselves to it will be the extent of the contortion of our true god-birthed image and identity—twisted, we will not work well! Neither will our chosen, changed, and believing children.

Speaking to the Father of those given to Him, Jesus prayed,

> "I have given them your word and the world has hated them, for they are not of the world any more than I am of the world. My prayer is not that you take them out of the world but that you protect them from the evil one. They are not of the world, even as I am not of it. Sanctify them by the truth; your word is truth. As you sent me into the world, I have sent them into the world." (John 17:14–18)

Wow. My Ellen. My Emma. In this world, it gets no better than them! But there isn't much in support of God's opinion of them.

Since our school system is not set up to accurately identify, separate, and equip attending believers and pagans, designing programs and curriculum to match (worship and sanctification for these, fear and conniving for those), it goes without saying that our schools have something else in view when thinking about our children. The big picture painted day after day for my daughters does not accurately reflect life for them, nor their fit with it. I don't mean to lay blame here; I do mean to illuminate. When our Christian children and young people are misidentified, it cannot be helped that they are mistreated. As if there were no deep difference between the two types populating the classrooms, our children are lumped together and identified as humans in need of skills for the life they can have—here's what you'll need. *We'll identify it for you.*

While I want my children to learn the three R's and to have a healthy immersion in music, history, philosophy, etc., I don't want them to believe that's it, "Now fit in and find your life-long career path! You can really be somebody if you'll go this way in the big picture we've set before you." That's the wrong-headed pursuit of trivial nobility, and it will lead them down a path of frustration. It doesn't fit with who they are.

So, Sarah and I are ramping up our discussions about the unseen nature of the frustrations they encounter. It keeps us believing what God thinks of our daughters (we see them!), and it's illuminating and practical for them. How we see them and what speaks most to us about them will determine how we treat them—it must.

I have spoken with hundreds of parents over the course of my life as a pastor and they would tell you that what made the biggest impact in their relationship with their children is when they saw them as God saw them. Prior to that when asked to describe their kids they would go on about what their children liked and disliked, how they behaved and didn't, and what some of their hopes and fears were. None of them said, "Well, Ashley is a female human who has B positive blood running through her veins, DNA which has produced brown hair and green eyes, a slight excess of teeth and a strong jaw, and a lineage which will probably cause her to excel in mathematics and have poor people skills. We believe she'll be quite happy working in a laboratory. Yep, that's our Ashley." No one ever told me of the composition of their children, the various components mixed together to produce what they were feeding and raising at home.

However, no one ever told me who their children were from God's perspective, either. "Well, Ashley is quite a lot like her Father. She's a righteous girl, full of the Spirit, and perfectly designed for His glory. We know that Ashley is of God and we're delighted to be her parents . . ." *His opinion* had not become *their opinion*; they were subject to and focused upon the Ashley they could see, rather than the Ashley who lived within.

121

As long as parents see their children as someone to raise and train, requiring shifting measures of love and compassion, sternness and strength, direction and discipline, they don't *see their kids*. Instead they see trainees, who require from them the just-right combination of leadership so they can grow up and be successful, happy, faithful, good. Therefore, the faith of the parents was wrapped-up in how they were doing with their trainee, Ashley, God's little ball of clay left to their charge.

If Ashley takes cookies without asking, correct her quickly so she'll know not to do that as an adult. Who knows, at seventeen she might be stealing Cadillacs if you don't. If she thanks mom for dinner and asks to be excused from the table, affirm her and praise her so she'll do that when dining at someone else's home also. If you don't, she might think you don't care and become a habitual dinnertime offender. If Ashley gets a little (or a lot) snippy with you, correct her on the spot so she'll know to respect adults. If you don't, Ashley might become a snippy snob for the rest of her life and have you to blame for it. Horrors!

Absolute vigilance is what's required and perfect, parental skills are the tool. Come to this class, read these books, go to that seminar, and you'll have what? *Good kids*. Which will mean what? *Good adults*. So what! That's not what they are and that's not nearly what they will become!

His purpose for them is far greater than that they get along in class, get good grades and jobs, or become upstanding citizens in a world in need of role models. His purpose and plan is much higher than that, and He has already changed them for that reason and to that end. They won't "get there" sometime after middle school or sometime post high school or when they've had a chance to get their college education and choose to enter the useful ranks of knowledgeable, well-prepared Christians when they're ready— *they've arrived*! And they're in a nasty, very confusing storm. By His grace and through the truth, our girls will know the nature of the storm in which they live. Yours should too.

Our kids are aliens—it's incredible—*and it's going to hurt*. Life for them has a built-in need for us. What pulls me into intimacy with my daughters is not the daily Bible reading I'm supposed to do with them and it's not the purposeful teaching on character, morals, or manners either. It's sharing in their uncomfortable and impossible fit in this world. I know the terrible struggle, I know the tempting lure, and now they do too.

It hurts. But it's a pain which keeps us from an assimilating dependence upon the false comforts and techniques of this world which would cover up and diminish our alienness. Knowing why our fit in this world hurts makes the pain understandable and perhaps tolerable. We aren't like it, we're not of it, so don't try to reverse the fact and overcome it. Instead, accept the glory of what it means and live as we are. The pain Sarah and I have is the very same pain Ellen and Emma have and it's there for a reason. When I forget, that pain eventually gets my attention so that I repent and go back for a reminder.

I can't just *treat* my kids as God would, I must *think* of my kids as God does. When I see what He sees, I fit with Him and feel it! When I do not, I give Him some work to do—on me. Our Christian children are aliens and we live together in a land that's not our own. If we can get that, our approach to them will be vastly different and uniquely invigorating, and it will keep us living on the edge of the visible and invisible, of temporal and eternal. And for us, that's pretty normal.

This world wants to keep us under wraps and keep us from knowing anything about who we actually are and keep our "alienness" impractical so it can go about its business. If successful, we remain undetected to ourselves, deceived from knowing how incredible and valuable we are.

That's the scheme against us and that's the scheme against our children. As soon as they're born again, their new identity marks them for the grace of God, but it also marks them as targets for the enemy—and he is merciless. The best strategy of the devil is the one least noticeable, the one which slowly ensnares its victim. Even better if the victim *likes the fit*.

While the Holy Spirit and Sarah and I work to raise them in the knowledge of God so they can really live, there is a carnival of activity vying for our girls' attention and allegiance. The big attractions are which television shows to watch (Disney or Animal Planet?), which fashions to wear, which recreational activities to choose, which video games to play, which foods to eat, and which boys to like, because visible life all around them demands attention.

The more opinionated my girls become about visible life ("American Idol *rocks*, Disney *stinks!*"), the less opinionated they become about invisible life. The more Ellen and Emma grow passionate about how to clothe themselves ("Sweatshirts are *in*, jackets are *out!*"), the less they care about the clothing they have already in Christ (Galatians 3:26-27). The more engrossed they become in what makes up the right boy, the right food, and the right game to play, the more deeply they dive into the pursuit of trivial nobility. That's the snare. As the visible world becomes the dominant, passion-lighter of life, the sons and daughters of God exchange true life for a fake. And the cover-up is complete. Getting them to make the proper exchange later can prove terribly difficult as their expectations have been lowered; their appetite for the bread of life has been stuffed with bread that does not satisfy.

The game for Sarah and me isn't won by dressing them in frumpy duds nor by forbidding them to like boys nor is it won by throwing the television into the trash. We believe we are working in concert with the Spirit when we are building them up in Christ, reminding them who they are, and pointing out what friction with this world really means—they are incredible aliens! We don't want that covered up. They're not *only human*, they're *alien*. It takes discipline to remember their "alienness," because the need and opportunity to properly identify and build them up in opposition to the lies sent by the devil is presented many times throughout the day.

If we're not careful to live by faith, we might begin to sow to the flesh of our kids. Yesterday Emma said, "Daddy, I'm a worrywart."

And here's what I thought: You know, *she is*. She's always got something negative to be concerned about, always some wrong or some bad that gets her attention. What a worrywart. I should tell her to trust God . . . As I prepared to blurt out a confirmation followed by a healthy prescription, I nevertheless took the briefest of pauses, hesitating ever so slightly to see if the Spirit might interject something. Lo and behold, He did.

"She's no worrywart. She's often plagued by it, but it's not her; it's something against her."

Shocked into the reality I cannot see, I said, "Emma, my girl, do you think that worry comes *from* you, or does it come *at* you?" Because I wanted her to think and, in so doing, sow to the Spirit, I said no more.

She answered, "It comes from the monster. It comes from my flesh. Then, Daddy, why do I worry so much?"

"Well," I replied, "it isn't your fault. Our monsters are really monstrous, aren't they? Everybody's is. But what you and I get to see is God in us, smacking the monster for us. Remember how to think or talk toward Him when you feel all that fight going on inside? It's fun to find Him in there, isn't it?" Pulling her onto my lap, I said, "Come on. Let's find Him inside together." She wiggled her little body into a comfortable spot, and I prayed, "Jesus, Emma and I believe You're in us right now. We feel the fight You're having with the monster. Would You put it in its place and would You do what You love to do in us, and make peace and trust and love more obvious than fear? Emma and I don't like the battle inside, but we know what to do about it. Thanks for living in us . . ."

And Emma said softly, "Amen." Think that was a good moment?

I don't want Emma to get overwhelmed by confusing her flesh with herself, which means I have to make that distinction too. That confusion is so destructive, the effects stretching out like roots to touch everything they can. Not only might she come to believe *she is* what God believes *she is not*, but she might come to act upon it and live out her days trying to conquer herself . . . or give in and give up. And that can stretch through families and friends—even to generations. So here's what we do:

First, Sarah and I believe that Ellen and Emma were chosen by God, and that makes all the difference. Because we believe it, we work with the Holy Spirit to help us maintain that belief, concerning ourselves and concerning our daughters. In our conversations and in prayer (together and apart), we regularly bring up the fact of our security because God chose us before He made anything or set any of it in motion (see Ephesians 1). We were His idea and we frequently return to awe, thankfulness, and rest because of that. It sets us right.

Everybody in our house has been made holy and blameless and has been set up for "the praise of His glorious grace" (Ephesians 1:6). We work to make certain that we remain impressed with God's grace to us in Christ. It flavors much of what we talk about, and believing it influences and gives power to all of our choices following. We live by faith in Him, and knowing that He chose us for Himself keeps us invigorated.

In my view, the church has been overemphasizing our need to choose God, and keep choosing Him in all we do. What it usually means is, "Kids! Do the right thing! Make good choices—*God is watching!*" Often it's simply a behavioral appeal—if kids think God is in the room, they'll be good. The church has been working so hard to get our children to make good choices that I don't think we're much impressed by God's choice of them. *So we don't marvel.* We don't wonder at our kids because we're not convinced that He is convinced they're so wonderful. We need to be.

Second, surface activity gets our attention, but it doesn't always reveal what's below. In 1980 I was visiting a number of churches, not knowing what I was looking for since I was a neophyte Christian. Sampling on Sundays gave me an important opportunity to see the incredible diversity amongst churches; their themes and theology, styles, and services were dramatically different and I didn't know what was right or what I wanted.

Sampling one Sunday, the pastor held up one of those plastic lemon-looking containers of lemon juice and said, "Christians are containers; squeeze them hard enough and what's inside will come out." The remainder of his sermon was all about making certain our behavior glorified God, no matter the squeeze life put upon us. Obviously, I've not forgotten his object lesson, but my opinion of it has changed.

I want to remember and to help my daughters know *it's not true.* Likening ourselves to a plastic lemon juice container or to a tube of toothpaste assumes there is only one item in the container; squeeze it and *whatever* comes out reveals the reality within.

Following that logic, if Ellen says something critical about Emma, that must mean Ellen is a critical person. And in the critical moment I might say, "You're such a critic, Ellen!" If Emma throws a tantrum because she's not getting her way, that must mean, "Emma, you're such a tantrum-throwing person!" Maybe I should follow it up with a nice, "Quit that and glorify God!" On the other hand, if one of them does a good deed, that must make her a good deed doer. "Oh, Ellen, my little good deed doer. Here's my approval, and while I'm at it, here's God's too . . ." And every day throughout the day, I wonder just who my kids are because I'm looking only at their surface.

Do you see what happens? It's not long before life in the Harris home is all about behavior! I am set up as Pharisee of the house, ever watchful and critical, the Judge of Behavior and Referee of Results. And since I'm doing so much, God has little to do. What a happy family *that* makes.

Our Christian children are not what they do, they're not how they behave, and they're not what they say—they're who God says they are. Without excusing poor, fleshly behavior, we must not allow it to sell the lie that our kids are how they look. When the surface looks particularly stormy, we must know that under the waves there is something amiss, something out of line, and *go there*. If our children's flesh is on display, in all of its ugly glory, rescue them! Revive them! Build them up in Christ, reminding them of how Christ has made them and that He is in them. If their behavior is stinky, it's usually because their thinking is too. You can help them and interrupt the game against them.

This is liable to seem so impractical and impossible, so pie-in-the-sky, but *only because we've never done it!* We're so immature here that we think it's impossible. And if we feel that it's impossible, then the scheme of the devil remains effective. But you *can* do it—you can interrupt the enemy's game plan.

As I've said before, sometimes you simply have to stop fleshly behavior immediately, "Jeremy! Stop this instant! You may NOT put that knife in your brother!" And you may not always stop the behavior *just right* either. That's another story. But after you've got the knife away from him, take a moment to address the heart. You may assume it is being held captive while the flesh does its thing.

Third, Sarah and I work to believe Ellen and Emma are in Christ, no matter what happens, regardless of their behavior. *That keeps us sane!* When life storms around them (or within them), we're kept from becoming too attracted to the storm of the moment and lost to what Jesus thinks and might like to do. When the storm blows in our family (from without or from within), the sinful desire which wars against my soul in the midst of the storm is to come away from knowing Jesus and offering myself to the Spirit for His grace and power and instead go out and control the storm. In other words, "do something" replaces "know Someone," and off I go. I'm not always quick to return either.

Have you noticed that seeing too quickly to the storm, you lose any knowledge of Christ in you—of who He is and what He has to offer? What becomes most captivating is the threat of the storm and the fear it brings out of your flesh, "Oh, no! Do something!" I'm reminded of the furious storm which blew up around that godly bunch gathered together in the boat on the lake. Ever find it strange that Jesus rebuked them for waking Him up because of the storm? The disciples had first given themselves to the storm instead of to the Lord, becoming engrossed in it and terrified. Who wouldn't? They hadn't forgotten that He was in the boat; they had simply become more attracted to and involved with the threat of the storm. The disciples' approach to Him was late and out of sequence. As usual, Jesus did something about it (hooray!), but they needlessly became subject to what they saw rather than who they knew. (See Mark 4:37-41.)

Every difficulty Ellen and Emma go through (or put us through), each triumph they achieve or failure they endure, they are still at all times in Christ and have everything because of it. Jesus is their strength; Jesus is their righteousness. Sarah and I work to keep that foremost in our thinking and approach. We work to keep that secure foundation in Ellen's and Emma's thinking as well. And we're careful to not send them a confusing, false message that they don't already have everything in Christ— they do! We want to be so positive about God's grace to us, that earning God's favor and blessing remain something Jesus already did for them and not something they have to do for themselves.

We know some will say we're giving them a license to abuse the grace of God. We believe we're holding them *to* His grace and keeping them in awe because of it. We'll take the risk.

Paul wrote:

> For *the grace of God* that brings salvation has appeared to all men. *It teaches us* to say "No" to ungodliness and worldly passions, and to live self-controlled, upright and godly lives in this present age, while we wait for the blessed hope—the glorious appearing of our great God and Savior, Jesus Christ, who gave himself for us to redeem us from all wickedness and to purify for himself a people that are his very own, eager to do what is good. (Titus 2:11-14, italics mine)

What is it which teaches our girls best? *The grace of God.* God's grace isn't only the *condition* in which we stand with Him, but God's grace is also the *power* by which He works in us. Knowing God and how well-off they are with Him through Christ *works* and *teaches* our girls to say "No" far better than any list we could come up with and drill into them.

Fourth, Sarah and I regularly talk with God about our girls, asking His opinion of them. He shows us that Ellen and Emma are godly already—right on course and right on time. When their behavior or experiences or thoughts expressed to us say something to the contrary, we believe nothing has changed. You may assume correctly that we talk with Him a lot!

If we don't ask Him to show us what He sees, we may begin to think God isn't doing anything with them; they're blocking Him. Someone or something is blocking Him; someone is to blame—so let's figure out who or what it is and get it fixed. We may begin to think of them as having a small inner compartment where God is hunkered down, cowering or embarrassed, instead of seeing them as at all times in Christ, chosen and happily indwelt by Him. And our relationship with them will be kept to the surface which has our attention, while what's underneath remains an impractical mystery.

In truth, however, Ellen and Emma aren't just on their way to heaven, they're already from it (see Ephesians 2:6). He is far more active with His children than we are! Because we don't always see it, *we ask.*

Further, we ask ourselves questions such as whether or not our girls are learning and getting Jesus from us, or if, because we just want them to be good, they're getting a heavy dose of the ten commandments. Are they getting shepherds who enjoy walking with them or Pharisees who walk with them only to keep them in line? One enjoys intimacy while the other sacrifices it for a proper performance. Are we truly enjoying our girls and are they truly enjoying us? If we get stung by these and other questions, we head into some focused time with God, who has the grace and love to set us aright.

But what if it doesn't work? What if our little aliens don't live by faith? What if they don't make the right choices and follow God—what then? Then we'll be living by faith in God—we've no other plan.

All these people were still living by faith when they died. They did not receive the things promised; they only saw them and welcomed them from a distance. And they admitted that they were aliens and strangers on earth. People who say such things show that they are looking for a country of their own. If they had been thinking of the country they had left, they would have had opportunity to return. Instead, they were longing for a better country—a heavenly one. Therefore God is not ashamed to be called their God, for he has prepared a city for them. (Hebrews 11:13-16)

Chapter Thirteen

The End of Pretending

*But we have this treasure in jars of clay to show
that this all-surpassing power is from God and
not from us. (2 Corinthians 4:7)*

There are lots of ways by which to know and feel and hear
and experience God. I've found that any way I can know Him
and find Him in me is worth it. And while I have my favorite
ways and fairly cling to them (wading in a mountain stream at
sunset while waving my fly rod would be one), there are some
that I'd rather avoid and just read about. These are the ones that
would not be my first choice, but they may be the most
important.

A friendship I had long trusted in went steadily wrong a few
years ago. No amount of phones calls and E-mails and meetings
and prayers could clean up the mess, so determined was my one-
time friend to cast me as his enemy. Not even my silence put out
the fires of accusation, and the ugly smears went on without me.
While it boggled my mind that there was nothing I could do, still
I tried and brooded on it, turning it over and over in my
thoughts, even in my sleep. I was terribly frustrated. It was the
ugliest battle of my life.

God was surely doing something, but I wanted Him to do
something else. I wanted Him to make things right, to trumpet
my innocence and integrity, and to do a great work in my friend's
heart. It didn't happen and I'm not holding my breath.

What did happen is that I found God in me—what I love
most through something I love least, personal anguish. Because I
had to, I turned to Him and looked for Him and listened for Him
and felt for Him and depended upon Him—and I knew God in
my terrible state of frustration. Months of ongoing battle went

past, and I understood anew what had at times been only theory: ". . . when I am weak, then I am strong" (2 Corinthians 12:10). I loved knowing God in that season, but I would still hesitate to sign my name when the "Who wants to be treated like Jesus?" volunteer list came around again.

My personal rallying cry has to be what Paul wrote to the Philippians in chapter three—I cannot get enough of knowing God. I remember the joy of discovering that knowing Him was truly my biggest thrill and greatest desire. I was so happy! But I also read that not only did my favorite mentor want to "know Christ and the power of his resurrection," but he added this little phrase, "and the fellowship of sharing in his sufferings" (Philippians 3:10). While my early days of delighting in Jesus went on and on, still that little tidbit occasionally haunted me. Jesus suffered a lot, I thought, it was sometimes horrible, it was always unjust, and it was often alone. My inner coward worked out an alternate route. Maybe if I have great integrity and solid character, work hard, and am really nice, fun, and good to have around, I'll escape that suffering part.

Riiiiiiiiiiiiiiight.

I don't like suffering. I have worked long hours at building a doctrine against it. Aren't I supposed to prosper in everything, be in good health, and have a fair portion of those "cows on a thousand hills?" Isn't that the deal? Isn't that what I got when I signed up?

When I first became a Christian the majority of the teaching I got was about how to work the spiritual system. You do it right, you get good things; you do it wrong and you get the opposite. Whatever happened that was good and prosperous and happy was God (proving you were doing something right), and whatever happened that was bad or ugly or frustrating was the devil (you were doing something wrong).

Simple. Work the system.

Because I wanted good, I worked hard to do the right things and began urging others to do the same. "God wants you to live well so it will go well with you, and here's how." Work the system. Simple. The only difficulty I was having was that I read my Bible. And when you've got neat and tidy, user-friendly doctrine like I did, you're going to be troubled by the Bible, especially when you hang out with Paul. "For it has been granted to you on behalf of Christ not only to believe on him, but also to suffer for him, since you are going through the same struggle you saw I had, and now hear that I still have" (Philippians 1:29-30).

Really, Paul, what a bother you are. If I had to listen to you, I wouldn't fall asleep and fall out a window like brother Eutychus—I'd *jump*.

Come on—*work the system*. Simple.

Unfortunately (or fortunately, depending upon how you look at it), I continued to read my Bible, and one day I stumbled across a passage which the Holy Spirit would use to forever upset my smug assessment of life.

In verse seven of the twelfth chapter of his second letter to the Corinthians, Paul wrote of an incredible time with God which essentially equipped him to be something of a know-it-all. Now knowing a lot isn't a bad thing, especially if one were to have the assignment of preacher to the Gentiles. Yet, after having an amazing, and no doubt satisfying, time with God, Paul writes, "To keep me from becoming conceited because of these surpassingly great revelations, there was given me a thorn in my flesh, a messenger of Satan, to torment me."

What? I thought. Where's the sense in that?

After a moment the following question popped into my mind: "Who would want to keep Paul from becoming conceited?"

Answering the sudden pop quiz I thought, Well, not the devil—he'd *want* Paul to become conceited. It must have been . . . *oh, no!* God gave Paul the thorn? God intentionally weakened Paul by giving him something demonic? Does that mean God was against Paul? It can't! As my tight theology began to unravel, I read on. "Three times I pleaded with the Lord to take it away from me. [Only three? What if Paul had asked a fourth time? Would that have worked?] But he said to me, 'My grace is sufficient for you, for my power is made perfect in weakness.' Therefore I will boast all the more gladly about my weaknesses, so that Christ's power may rest on me. [God wanted Paul and He wants me . . . WEAK! And He works in my life so that *happens*?!] That is why, for Christ's sake, I delight in weaknesses, in insults, in hardships, in persecutions, in difficulties. *For when I am weak, then I am strong*" (2 Corinthians 12:7-10, italics mine).

Oh, no. This changes everything, I thought. And I was right. That day I backed up and read the entire book of 2 Corinthians in one sitting. I vividly remember feeling painfully refreshed, as though my brain had just been slapped with after shave. "Thanks. I *needed* that." After my Corinthian glut, I wrote the following in the empty margin of the last chapter: "God will not rest until you do. He will burn you out."

Sooner or later you're going to come up against a terrible weakness you cannot avoid—the lure of alcohol or pornography or cheating or gorging or coveting that is too strong to resist. It will be a frustrating inability you're unable to conquer, an unjust accusation which won't go away, a public insult which marks you and wounds deeply, an impossible hardship or a difficulty you cannot weather, and you'll cry out to God to rescue you . . . and He won't. You'll still have the weakness, you'll still stumble, your situation won't change, you won't receive an apology, and things will remain unbearably difficult. And you'll be right on time.

In virtually any kind of suffering, God works in us to bring out what He put in, the very life of Christ. God lives in us and, while it's a pleasure to find Him there in safety and prosperity, it is at least as important to find Him there in calamity and poverty. It's terrific to have God at a party where everyone is celebrating, but how much better to have Him at a disaster where pain and chaos reign? Think how He would stand out.

And that's what He likes.

I want to live by faith in what Jesus said is true about situations and people, good and bad; those that are His and those that are not yet. Living by faith means that I believe and choose to carry out the kind of actions in keeping with it, including trusting Him and treating others in a manner which glorifies God. The energy necessary for the acts is the beginning point of finding Christ in us.

We're prone to pretending, you and I, acting as though we're capable when the truth is *that's* not the issue. God has not invested Himself in our capability but in His own! And He wants you and me to have that. God is not willing that we should be kept from the authentic life and grace of Christ in us, so He allows—even causes—awful frustration to visit with us.

This isn't about learning and growing either. Once you've found Christ's power at work within you through frustration, it doesn't mean you've passed the class and there will be no more tests. What a crazy thought that is; we expect that growing in Christ means life gets better with time, passing one class and grade after another, and one day we'll graduate. That's not what this is. This is where belief and experience meet, where life is less and less about pretending and posturing and more and more about the reality of Christ in us. Paul's life experiences didn't get better and nicer or become mellow with age. He didn't proclaim that he wanted to be done with this life and get on to the next because he was bored but because he ached. (See 2 Corinthians 5.)

Prolonged frustration and bother don't happen simply to goad us into good behavior or to "teach us a lesson"—it keeps us from pretending we can do anything apart from Christ. And it happens so we'll find Him. The inability to keep yourself together or to keep producing the look of love for someone for whom you feel none is not a sign that you need to recommit and do the right thing. It's the death of thinking you can and are supposed to do anything apart from Jesus. Frustration is the beginning of the end of pretending.

Too often we fail to think of ourselves as *in Christ*, living in Him at every moment. Instead we think of ourselves as outside of Christ with a whole lot to do for Him. We may think of quiet times and moments of solitude with Jesus as charging up our depleted batteries; better not let yours run down too far or your whole system will crash. Plug in, charge up, and off you go, hoping you're charged-up enough to face the unknown of the day. And when it appears you're not, keep smiling, hold it together, and pretend anyway. Wouldn't Jesus *want* it that way?

No, He wouldn't. In light of your inability, instead He would beckon you to live by faith that He is within and that He is capable. That's why frustration is so important! It keeps us bothered with this world and the stuff we go through every day so we'll not live by it or for it. When you've grown discontented with the world, a look within will save you from a needless burnout.

Jesus said:

"Remain in me, and I will remain in you. No branch can bear fruit by itself; it must remain in the vine. Neither can you bear fruit unless you remain in me. I am the vine; you are the branches. If a man remains in me and I in him, he will bear much fruit; apart from me you can do nothing. If anyone does not remain in me, he is *like* a branch that is thrown away and withers; such branches are picked up, thrown into the fire and burned. If you remain in me and my words remain in you, ask whatever you wish, and it will be given you. This is to my Father's glory, that you bear much fruit, showing yourselves to be my disciples." (John 15:4-8, italics mine)

When we try to do much apart from Him, we become "like a branch," which is good only for the fireplace. We're just heat that passes away.

How many times have you witnessed (or experienced) someone doing a lot for the Lord, someone really "on fire," only to watch them undergo burnout? Usually the fire doesn't die out in a moment but over a season of time. There are flare-ups here and there, occasional bursts of heat, but they happen less and less often until you could say "their fire's out." No matter how the hearth is poked and prodded by the pastor or by friends, the heat is gone. They're like a dry branch.

That's when one of two things happens: some who have grown heatless will settle and grow accustomed to their state and say, "Well, the honeymoon had to end sometime, didn't it?" Sometimes they continue to fairly regularly fill their seat on Sunday, smiling and responding appropriately, departing with a look of satisfaction. They've learned to get by and to deal with the sad lack of heat, now mostly a haunting memory. They'd like more, but getting their hopes up will just lead to disappointment, so they don't muster the strength they think is required. They're present, but there ain't much heat.

On the other hand, many of the burned-out evacuate the building, limping off disappointed and disillusioned. Someone failed—either them or someone in authority— and, confused as to where to put the blame, they slink off never to be heard from again. Why should they be subjected to one more exhortation of "Here's what you've gotta do for God" when either it doesn't work or they don't? Having heard their share of sermons as to how to get or act busy as if they had fire and heat when, in fact, they don't, they weary of pretending. These are the ones who, when asked why they left the church, tell you that "everyone there was a bunch of actors and I can't do that anymore." To them going to church is like joining the screen actors guild in which some who have joined can do well ("I can act!"), but others like themselves refuse the stage ("I can't do that!") and wander off dejected. That's what these do. In either case, it's cold because the fire's out.

Burnout is all around us. When I speak of burnout I don't mean that the limited amount of fuel in the fireplace of our heart has been consumed, so let's get it replaced, let's get that fire burning again, wiser and smarter, with more potential for a long burn. What I mean is that one kind of fuel has finally been exhausted—burned-out—and it's time for a *new kind of fuel* altogether. God Himself is the fuel for our life.

Today the media is crammed full of information about alternative fuels. From uniting gasoline and big batteries in our hybrid cars to finding new ways to energize our lives, fuel for energy is everything. "Can't stay awake at work? Nodding off too soon? Drink this potion, pop this pill, eat this energy bar, do this workout and voila! Strength!" But that kind of strength can become a substitute, a stand-in, for true strength from God and it won't work, even if we think it will.

So, because God knows who we have become, He works to exhaust our singular reliance upon false or insufficient resources (charisma, style, eloquence, talent, strength, etc.) so that He can be found and formed in us, and then be visible through us. What's more exciting than that? And He does it regardless of whether or not we recognize His effort—with or without our permission. *And* He will use just about anything in our life to bring it to pass, including pressure and conflict and disappointment on the job or at church or with a spouse, physical frustrations, heavy burdens, relational craziness, even a messenger of Satan. Out of gas? Feeling exhausted? That's *good*.

It's time for a new fuel source. God is that faithful and we desperately need Him to be.

Just when you would think God would pave the way and make things easy for Paul, the opposite occurs. Out preaching the Gospel, Paul writes, "We do not want you to be uninformed, brothers, about the hardships we suffered in the province of Asia. We were under great pressure, far beyond our ability to endure, so that we despaired even of life. Indeed, in our hearts we felt the sentence of death. *But this happened that we might not rely on ourselves but on God, who raises the dead*" (2 Corinthians 1:8-9, italics mine).

Paul, do you mean it happened on purpose? Yes. Did God have something to do with it? Yes, again. God will so orchestrate things in our lives that we cannot cope, notwithstanding the energy drinks and alcohol and pornography and drugs and recreation and therapies which we use to medicate ourselves. He is *not* punishing us! Nor has the devil broken through God's protective boundary unauthorized, now to ravage our lives and plans. This is not a call to "suck it up" and to muster the proper strength so God can do something but an invitation to proper weakness, "so that Christ's power may rest on me" (2 Corinthians 12:9). Only then is God's grace discovered to be entirely sufficient!

God had set Paul up to find Christ within and He was working with Paul so he would. That usually takes some doing.

My Christian history shows that I don't quickly embrace weakness in order to find God. If the Spirit sent me an early morning E-mail about my day which read, "Good news, Ralph! Today will be a terrific day of weakness—you'll have opportunities galore!" I think I would come down suddenly with the flu and jump back in bed! I would rely upon fleshly resources and, looking out at my day, fail to look within. And that day Christ would not be found in me because I would have found an alternate way to live and cope—stay home.

Have you ever done something like that? Have you ever been faced with an upcoming meeting you knew would be difficult and, rather than look and listen for God in you, given everything you had to be properly prepared? You know, dressed and psyched yourself up, put your name on the prayer line, planned out several options, and crossed your fingers so you could handle anything and everything? How did you feel afterward? Exhausted? You burned the wrong fuel.

God thinks He lives in you and that you would love to find Him there, reducing your stress by relegating you to more of a spectator than an initiator. God is carrying on the process which will get you off the demanding stage of life, taking away all the pressure you feel to come up with today's best act and resources to match, so that He can provide what He is like in you! In essence, He is working for intimacy with you and intimacy with the world through you! Everybody gets Him.

This is how God treats us not as sons only, but as vessels for Himself, holy containers for His show. God didn't make me and choose me so I will do well but so He will do well, and He made me and chose me so that will be obvious. That's the part that makes me feel like it's not always a good idea to cuddle up with God. My flesh, recoiling with horror, makes itself felt. Quick! Do something! Say something! Don't be a coward and do nothing—move! But more and more I'm learning to prefer what God thinks and to prefer what I will find when I look to where He is found. That may seem foolish and weak in the opinion of this world, but I'm no longer of it and I know better.

Besides, God has been choosing the foolish and the weak for a long, long time. He didn't stop before He picked us either, so you know what that means—count us in the crowd. Why would He do that? Well, where would God be most visible and obvious? Wouldn't it be where things are tough? Wouldn't it be in situations and circumstances where, in contrast with how things appear, He would stand out?

Paul wrote:

> For God, who said, "Let light shine out of darkness," made his light shine in our hearts to give us the light of the knowledge of the glory of God in the face of Christ. *But we have this treasure in jars of clay to show that this all-surpassing power is from God and not from us.* (2 Corinthians 4:6-7 italics mine)

Just try thinking of God lurking in a planter and you've got the picture. Should the pot attempt to be strong and capable, summon its mineral resources and put on a show? No! It should take every opportunity to fall over! It doesn't have a mouth so it can't invite anyone to take a peek inside ("Well, look what's here!"), it doesn't have talent so it can't dazzle anyone enough to prove what's there, and it certainly can't defend itself against a hammer—"Boy! We've given you a dozen whacks and you haven't cracked; God must live in there!" It's not that we actually *are* a jar of clay, but, figuratively speaking, we have one within us. Now that God lives there, every knock and smack on us is an invitation not to parade the pot but to crack or tip over letting out the treasure! The whack on the pot will happen again and again, like it or not, because God loves to work through you and me. We get delight ("God is in me!") and others get the life of God.

> We are hard pressed on every side, but not crushed; perplexed, but not in despair; persecuted, but not abandoned; struck down, but not destroyed. We always carry around in our body the death of Jesus, so that the life of Jesus may also be revealed in our body. For we who are alive are *always* being given over to death for Jesus' sake, *so that his life may be revealed in our mortal body.* So then, death is at work in us, but life is at work in you. (2 Corinthians 4:8-12, italics mine)

Doesn't this shed light on why things happen the way they do? He's moving us from one resource to another. In exhausting our natural resources so we can live by faith (call it *brokenness* if you must), He is carrying on with the sanctification of His sons and daughters. God is orchestrating for your life and His life to meet! When we know what He is doing, we can look through the temporary and visible circumstances and live by faith, finding the grace and energy of Christ in us.

I think Paul majored in this. Wanna serve Jesus? Consider Paul. His life of serving the Lord included being whipped with thirty-nine lashes on five different occasions, bobbing around in the ocean for a day and a half, being beaten with rods three different times, being shipwrecked five times (Get your tickets now to join Paul on his next glorious voyage to Israel!), being stoned by a mob, and being on the wrong side of jail bars! I tend to whine and fuss about my life not going the way I want if a publisher rejects my manuscript or if my car doesn't start immediately but Paul saw life differently. He was better off because he did.

Some people think of themselves as though they are a stubborn and resistant piece of cement that God can hardly wait to break. "Jesus! Do whatever it takes to break Ralph Harris; he's just so hard hearted. I can't use him until he's broken!"

"Yes, Father, I see what you mean. I'll work up a plan and get the angels on it right away. He's a tough one but we'll get it done."

Those who think this way often explain the circumstances of their days along these lines, as though the One who had rescued them was now the One resisting them. Rubbish. Everyone born again by the Spirit has been born of a new nature, and has everything in keeping with the terrific new creation they have become. At the core of their being, they will never again be unyielding pavement, nor will they have a rebellious spirit, nor will they need to be broken. If believers believe that they have a rock for a heart, then they will interpret most every hardship or difficulty in their day as God working to bust them a good one, getting their attention and securing their allegiance. "Knock that off, son! Or I'll *really* give it to you next time!"

Sometimes I give my dog a boot to her backside, sending her a message, but *she's a dog* and we do not speak the same language, nor do we have the same nature, nor do I live in her! I may get the behavior I want (and the lowered head and tail between the legs, as well) but so what? Do I get any glory for what I've done? Any worship or praise? Is she glad and thankful for the boot? No! She just wants to do whatever it takes to avoid it in the future. Is that how God treats us—like His special pack of dogs? That's a dog's life but it's not mine and it's not yours!

Some in the western church think that in order to get God the notice He deserves, we ought to throw Him a parade, one after the other, with blaring bands, cheerleaders, and oversized balloons. And as we march by, decked out and heads held high, those along the parade route (and those watching on TV) will certainly witness the glory of God in our splendor. Right? When the parade watchers see how good and clean we look, how well we march, and how tightly we keep our formation, they'll want to join in too. So we've got to practice our moves and work on our routines so that when it comes time for the show, we'll be ready and hit the right notes—be prepared, be strong, have it together.

Only that's not how it works.

For as long as I've been involved in ministry, I have experienced the competing desires of the parade versus the power of the kingdom. While I expect disagreement on this point, they do *not* get along. Almost without exception, where people are best met and changed by God Himself is not during the glamour and power of the parade but in the privacy of failure, in the awfulness of weakness, and in the torment of frustration. That's where God is and the people who know Him best find Him there and continue to visit.

Hardship and suffering and trials in the life of a Christian do not arrive because we're bad but because we're good (see James 1:2-4; 1 Peter 1:6-9; 4:12-19), and God is at work showing everyone just how good He has made us. God, who lives within us, loves to put Himself on display through the behavior of His vessels. While some will disagree, I don't believe that God rebukes believers for sins they've committed by trashing their days, but by directly speaking to them about it. If we sow to the flesh, we will reap from the flesh the junk Paul lists in Galatians 5, but we won't be reaping it from God. Naturally, if I spend my days in pajamas drinking bourbon, watching television, and cussing out the neighbors, my life will be miserable. But it won't be my Father making me miserable—it will be the flesh! As soon as I wake up from my worldly stupor and repent, God takes up the recovery of His sloppy-behaving son. He's really great with prodigals and the temporarily insane—He's amazing.

This keeps us from losing hope and letting go of faith and desire for God when the situations and circumstances of our lives are not what we would like them to be. Isn't that incredibly important? If we think we're the ones responsible for all the hardships, why bother turning to God for any insight and encouragement? What's He going to say? "Too bad about all that frustration. Better resolve yourself to unending misery, you big loser."

But that's not what's going on.

> Therefore we do not lose heart. Though outwardly we are wasting away, yet inwardly we are being renewed day by day. For our light and momentary troubles *are achieving for us* an eternal glory that far outweighs them all. So we fix our eyes not on what is seen, but on what is unseen. For what is seen is temporary, but what is unseen is eternal. (2 Corinthians 4:16-18, italics mine)

"Light and momentary troubles" don't arrive simply because you've failed or because God is mad at you or because the devil is on the loose. Even if you've messed up mountainously and are reaping what you've sown to the flesh, still your foolishness and weaknesses are the parade opportunities for the Lord Jesus. Try to eradicate them from your life and you'll compound them! Look through them, see them for the whacks on the pot that they are and, sewing to the Spirit by looking within, you'll decline the energy you're tempted to muster for the strength and ability He has.

And you won't be pretending. You'll come to like recognizing your weakness because you'll find the energy and life you're meant to have—Jesus Christ in you, the hope of glory!

> Dear friends, do not be surprised at the painful trial you are suffering, as though something strange were happening to you. But rejoice that you participate in the sufferings of Christ, so that you may be overjoyed when his glory is revealed. (1 Peter 4:12-13)

Chapter Fourteen

Taking Heaven With You

"The kingdom of heaven is like treasure hidden in a field. When a man found it, he hid it again, and then in his joy went and sold all he had and bought that field." (Matthew 13:44)

When I was in grade school I became increasingly aware of, and sometimes uncomfortable with, the fact that people had opinions about me. It all began when it was obvious that a girl *liked* me. Annalise approached my kingdom in the school sandbox during lunch time with more in mind than a comment about my stately castle and moat. I think my layout had clarified for her what she wanted in life—*me*. "We're going to get married and I'm going to buy you a watch and t-shirt," she proclaimed.

I stared at my castle. Annalise remained at my side, humming a pleasant tune in keeping with her romantic vision. Fortunately, the school bell rang, interrupting her blissful dream but providing a merciful escape for me. "Well, bye," I uttered.

I don't think I broke her heart, but I sure discovered something of my own. Annalise woke me up. I suddenly noticed that my teacher, Mrs. Van Duker, liked me and, as my astute eight-year-old daughter once said, "I like people who like me." It made me feel good. And then there was Heidi. I thought she was the most beautiful third grader in the world and that made me want her to think I was beautiful too. I remember how I felt when she did. What a validation it was—beauty recognizing beauty. It made my heart sing.

Consider what you've found through the pages of this book and how you've felt as a result. In contrast to what you once thought about yourself, don't you now feel better off? Why? Because now you're looking in the right place. You've swapped this world's opinion of yourself for God's view and it's changing your life. Hopefully, you've found a new and holy craving to know God and are learning that satisfying it is a wonderful labor of faith. Not only is His opinion of you true and better by far than any you've ever known, but knowing it does something to you! If God, who is perfect beauty, affirms *you as beauty*, your life changes dramatically and your heart sings! And it won't be a solo; your song will join the adoring chorus of the heavenly choir now thundering their delight and awe of God.

> And they sang a new song: "You are worthy to take the scroll and to open its seals, because you were slain, and with your blood you purchased men for God from every tribe and language and people and nation. *You have made them to be a kingdom and priests to serve our God, and they will reign on the earth.*" Then I looked and heard the voice of many angels, numbering thousands upon thousands, and ten thousand times ten thousand. They encircled the throne and the living creatures and the elders. In a loud voice they sang: "Worthy is the Lamb, who was slain, to receive power and wealth and wisdom and strength and honor and glory and praise!" Then I heard every creature in heaven and on earth and under the earth and on the sea, and all that is in them, singing: "To him who sits on the throne and to the Lamb be praise and honor and glory and power, for ever and ever!" (Revelations 5:9-13, italics mine.)

Heaven is singing! And why? Because of what God has made of you! Looking out over men and women and boys and girls who are made sons of God, all those in heaven are wild with ecstasy! They see the glory of God in the vessels of His grace and they're singing with abandoned glee. They recognize beauty in us. This is heaven's view of you and me, and this is heaven's response to the One who made it so! The rest of your life will be about the growing confidence and grace you gain by accepting heaven's view as reality and living from it—made in His image, sharing in His glory, once a beast, now beauty recognizing beauty. Incredible! Amazing!

I remember tossing my delighted and squealing daughters up into the air and catching them, only to hear them exclaim, "Do it again, Daddy! Do it again!"

And I think the angels are saying something similar as they watch in wonder as God changes another person into a holy dwelling place for Himself. "Incredible! Do it again, Father! Do it again!"

The four living creatures, the twenty-four elders, and the thousands and thousands of angels gathered together in joyful adoration are celebrating Jesus and what He has done with you and me. They are jubilant because they see the astonishing goodness of God in His outrageous grace to us. They simply can't get over the display of God's largesse in vessels so inherently unworthy—what a thrill! "Incredible! Do it again!" The angels know what we must know. And the angels are focused where we must focus.

All those in heaven see earth as the stage for God, and those of the heavenlies never become so transfixed by what happens on the stage that they quit looking at the Conductor. They're fascinated with Him! The amazing creatures and angels only glance at you and me and stare at God, marveling at His grace. And that's where our gaze should go also. Rejoice over those whom God has made righteous and holy but become transfixed by the One who made them that way. Looking to Him who is unseen, you will be convinced and refreshed by what is really true!

That's why we fix our thoughts and hearts on things above, in the heavens, and not on earthly things (Colossians 3:1-4). We don't do it so we'll feel better about ourselves and have a nice day, we do it because that's where we're made visible and our desire for the beauty who made us beautiful is satisfied. And we ought to be satisfied by Him again and again! We should seek our own satisfaction and delight in God, to be as happy as we can in Him, just as it is in heaven.

As C.S. Lewis has it, this is vitally important. "If there lurks in most modern minds the notion that to desire our own good and earnestly to hope for the enjoyment of it is a bad thing, I submit that this notion has crept in from Kant and the Stoics and is no part of the Christian faith. Indeed, if we consider the unblushing promises of reward and the staggering nature of the rewards promised in the Gospels, it would seem that our Lord finds our desires, not too strong, but too weak. We are half-hearted creatures, fooling about with drink and sex and ambition when infinite joy is offered us, like an ignorant child who wants to go on making mud pies in a slum because he cannot imagine what is meant by the offer of a holiday at the sea. We are far too easily pleased." (C.S. Lewis, "The Weight of Glory" *The Weight of Glory and Other Essays* Grand Rapids: Eerdmans, 1965, pp.1-2.)

The command, "Delight yourself in the Lord" (Psalm 37:4), is not a command to dance about and make merry as though the look of delight fulfills the command, but it's a directive unto our own enjoyment! When we find God to be our greatest joy and pleasure, the presumed pleasures of drink and sex and ambition and covetousness are exposed as the empty pretenders they are, and their grip upon us is loosened.

When I discovered the crazy love and joy I received from communion with God, I began gladly trading the many worldly pleasures for the one. It took little calculation on my part because I had so much delight. No one needed to tell me that bar-hopping, drink-pounding, and women-chasing on Saturday night violated God's commands and must be stopped for the glory of God. I found that He is truly delightful and pleasurable to be with (just as He says) and Saturday night carousing ceased to be the fun it once was. Even a little of it was like skipping any stages of fun and going right to the hangover on Sunday morning! Besides, what glory is in it for God if I cease Saturday night binging, not out of finding Him actually glorious and worthy and better but out of presumed duty? I would not have discovered anything good about God except that He's a demanding kill-joy, and there's no glory in that—neither is it true. And since God has wired me (and everyone) to seek and to find pleasure and satisfaction, when I don't find either after denying myself what little I had, I will come to resent Him—and begin sinning again.

John Piper writes, "Worship is a way of gladly reflecting back to God the radiance of His worth. This cannot be done by mere acts of duty . . . Consider the analogy of a wedding anniversary. Mine is on December 21. Suppose on this day I bring home a dozen long-stemmed red roses for Noel. When she meets me at the door I hold out the roses, and she says, 'O Johnny, they're beautiful, thank you,' and gives me a big hug. Then suppose I hold up my hand and say matter-of-factly, 'Don't mention it; it's my duty.' What happens? Is not the exercise of duty a noble thing? Do not we honor those we dutifully serve? Not much. Not if there's no heart in it. *Dutiful roses are a contradiction in terms . . .* In fact they belittle her. They are a very thin covering for the fact that she does not have the worth or beauty in my eyes to kindle affection. All I can muster is a calculated expression of marital duty." (*Desiring God: Meditations of a Christian Hedonist*, Multnomah Press, 1986, pp. 72-73, italics mine.)

When and if we're reduced to empty-hearted displays of affection for God, we subtly begin believing that He likes the display even if we don't. And what often comes from that point is a detrimental style of living that many call normal, where the show of worship and obedience goes on while our hearts are far off. In other words, we do things to please Him, but we remain unaware and without the benefit of knowing and sharing in His pleasure. And the distance grows from there as does the lifestyle.

Just yesterday I was in one of those draggy funks, where nothing was particularly bad and nothing was particularly good, but I felt a bout of "zombieness" had come over me. Looking in the mirror I saw a body with skin and hair and eyes, but seemingly without any blood or muscle to get the whole thing going. "What a stiff," I thought. "Oh, well. I've got work to do." As I turned to leave and launch into work, the Spirit interrupted the course of my thinking with two words: "*Delight yourself.*"

Now since God has proven Himself to be my treasure and greatest delight, I knew immediately that He was directing me toward a revival by enjoying God. I'll bet He has with you too. So His command, "*Delight yourself,*" directed me to Him so that I could share in the perspective of heaven which remains in glad awe of God. He is always on display there and what He thinks and does drives everybody nuts with joy. Nobody there makes the attempt to be or look happy nor do they concern themselves with their attitude—they look at Him and that's sufficient!

Looking at myself in the mirror, I saw confirming evidence of why I felt lifeless. Redirecting my gaze toward heaven's view did something about it! My flesh conspired against me to keep me visibly oriented so I would sow toward it—Man! I'll bet I've got zombie breath to match. Oh, well. I've got work to do. The flesh might have furthered the course by suggesting, There's no time to seek God. Just be faithful to do the work at hand the best you can. God likes faithfulness . . . Following that course, I might have breathed out an empty-hearted prayer and remained in the weariness that had my attention. Fortunately, the Spirit broke up the conspiracy, redirecting my perspective toward heaven's view and wooed me back to the proper vision for a son of God. "O Father. What are your thoughts today? What's happening with you?" I asked aloud. And in about ten seconds I looked like heaven.

I had a revival in my bathroom. And it wasn't like I was given an injection good for a few hours of strength, but the cover this world puts over heaven was removed and I could see again, see my fit, and see my Love! Living again by faith and filled with the Spirit, I went into the work of the day taking heaven with me. *I could see clearly.*

Heaven is celebrating God's grace to us in Christ. Returning over and over again to heaven's view and focus is the most vital and invigorating workout you and I will undertake—it's worth everything! Celebrating God's grace to us is essentially this— "Father, we believe and are staggered by the fact that you have given us *everything* for *nothing*. And you always will. Incredible! Astounding! To you who sit on the throne and to the Lamb be praise and honor and glory and power, for ever and ever!"

We can't get over it, and why should we! If God's grace and glory to us is the thrill of heaven, why shouldn't it be ours? It is! And finding virtually any way to remind yourself and others that He has given us *everything* for *nothing* is the way to the best of life and the best of you. It's how you live by faith.

An expert on how to live after dying to this world, Paul writes:

> *For the grace of God* that brings salvation has appeared to all men. *It teaches us* to say "No" to ungodliness and worldly passions, and to live self-controlled, upright and godly lives in this present age. (Titus 2:11-12, italics mine)

As we saw in Chapter 12, it isn't a list of do's and don'ts which teaches and equips us best toward righteous living, neither is it an accountability group so your feet can be held to the fire. And no, it isn't forcing oneself to surrender and do the will of God. What makes for the best of life is looking upon the magnificence of God! That heavenly view stimulates faith which is how we live—by faith. Any other manner trips up the Christian by dragging his focus from heaven's view and diverting it to an earthly one. And so the stumbling begins.

That's what happened to the Galatians. Having been given everything for nothing and having received the Holy Spirit, the guarantor or underwriter of every promise, still the Christians at Galatia were losing focus and taking a different view. They were falling from wonder and they were *falling from grace*.

Those who denied that Christians had been given everything for nothing in Christ had stealthily crept in to introduce old ways, former ways of securing God's favor. What turned Galatian heads was the lie that they didn't have His favor and blessing already in Christ but could have it if they would add to their faith a few practices—just a few rituals from the past. Then they would be even better off. Then God would really give them the grace and blessing and life they'd dreamed about.

Do you see the lie? Even though they were in Christ, new creations and sons of God, these "bewitchers" suggested the Galatians' condition with God had not been made perfect; His death on the cross was insufficient, His resurrection only partially securing a new day and new covenant! Sure, Jesus did *most* of the work, but here's what remains. Do this and do that, He'll see you do it, and the blessings of heaven will be yours. Fail to do this and do that and well, you know what history shows— it won't be pretty. And just look at your behavior; you know you don't live as you should. You don't think God will bless you living the way you are, do you? In other words, look at yourself outside of Christ, take an earthly view, and get with it! Start doing what God requires so He won't cut you off from His blessings. And these wicked workers dragged the former covenant into the new, creating a twisted and unrecognizable monstrosity. How gruesome it is when a Christian attempts to live by the former covenant.

The apostle Paul, overwhelmed with grief and righteous anger at those who would rob God of His glory in Christ, wrote: "Does God give you his Spirit and work miracles among you because you observe the law, or because you believe what you heard?" (Galatians 3:5).

Wake up, Galatians! You've got everything for nothing simply because you believe in what Christ has done! You've accepted heaven's view and you're astonishingly well-off because of it. You're free from the fear of thinking that God determines His treatment of you based upon your ability to earn it. He has made you sons in perfect standing! Don't let those bewitchers make you into slaves by agreeing to their miserable principles—they're worse than useless! And have you noticed that your joy is missing? It's gone because you've forgotten God's opinion of you, and you've accepted the opinion of someone else. And now you're believing and following men who want you to do what *they* think is best. They may be motivating you, but they're making you into something tragic—sons of God who don't believe what their Father believes! *How can you go forward in Christ?*

Because the glory of God was at stake, that twist was driving Paul crazy. So by the Spirit he writes:

> It is for freedom that Christ has set us free. *Stand firm,* then, and do not let yourselves be burdened again by a yoke of slavery. Mark my words! I, Paul, tell you that if you let yourselves be circumcised, *Christ will be of no value to you at all.* Again I declare to every man who lets himself be circumcised that he is obligated to obey the whole law. You who are trying to be justified by law have been alienated from Christ; *you have fallen away from grace.* But by faith we eagerly await through the Spirit the righteousness for which we hope. For in Christ Jesus neither circumcision nor uncircumcision has any value. The only thing that counts is faith expressing itself through love. (Galatians 5:1-6, italics mine)

By attempting to earn God's approval and favor (verse 4), the Galatian Christians had "been alienated from Jesus," or *stuck in neutral.* No matter how diligently they worked, no matter how much they revved their motors and honked their horns, urged on by the bewitchers, they couldn't move. And out of anguished love, Paul was calling them to return to faith in Jesus and how well-off they were because of Him. Only that would secure them and give them confidence to approach God's throne of grace, expecting to receive what He had already earned! (See Hebrews 4:16.)

Would God actually make the Galatians "a kingdom and priests," give them the Holy Spirit, do wonders, "and work miracles" simply because they believed? Shouldn't there be more to it? *No!* There isn't more, that's it! It's astounding—praise God! Everyone in heaven was praising Him for it, but the Galatians were chasing after the demonic lure of adding *something lacking* to the *everything they had for nothing.*

Has the devil dragged the Galatian lure by your nose lately? Because they bit on it, the Galatians suffered terribly, and so do we if we're fooled.

My brother, my sister, no matter how that lure comes and no matter who throws it by you, quickly look away from it to heaven's view of things . . . and do not bite. Ignore the lie by preferring the truth. Wherever you go, take heaven's view with you—keep it close! As prevalent as the lie is today, that will take some doing.

Among some there exists a misunderstanding of what living by grace entails for the Christian. These may think that "grace livers" don't do anything but ever wait upon the motivational *push* of the Spirit. While perhaps fairly characterizing them as reluctant to live by any rules by which they might become *more* holy, *more* righteous, or "*more better,*" others fail to see what great efforts "grace livers" make every day.

The fact and effectiveness of God's grace to us in Christ does not mean we do not make real and serious choices about life and about what we do daily. To the contrary, God's grace means that not only do we get to revel in Christ, finding His life within and ourselves animated because of it, but *we choose* to revel in Christ. In truth, that choice becomes our single most important act of faith.

So then, just as you received Christ Jesus as Lord, continue to live in him, rooted and built up in him, strengthened in the faith as you were taught, and overflowing with thankfulness. See to it that no one takes you captive through hollow and deceptive philosophy, which depends on human tradition and the basic principles of this world rather than on Christ. For in Christ all the fullness of the Deity lives in bodily form, and you have been given fullness in Christ, who is the head over every power and authority. (Colossians 2:6-10)

If we are to have the grace of God at work within us, then, aside from those marvelous times in which the Spirit sovereignly and surprisingly wells up within us toward some effect, we must do lots of things in keeping with the new life we now have, "stimulating" our true selves. *Inactivity* can easily become the *enemy of grace.*

If the believer just waits around for the Spirit's activity or motivation, kicking back and doing nothing with what He knows about the kingdom within him, then his problem isn't laziness—it's unbelief. Whether he has been overwhelmed or underwhelmed by the circumstances of life, unbelief has crept in and taken him captive. He's miserable because of it. The good news is that the Christian can have the best of life at any point by choosing to live in Christ. A reviving fullness greets us whenever we overcome creeping unbelief by remembering all we have been given in Him.

Sometimes when my efforts or hopes have taken a beating, and lethargy or disappointment threatens to seize me, I'll take a walk and verbalize all that is mine in Christ. As I talk aloud about having His righteousness and His holiness, what's often revealed is that I've begun to rely upon my own works as my righteousness and holiness—my own seal of approval. That will never do! So I make the choice to see myself *where I am* and *as I am*—in Christ, having all things. And that choice to give thanks restores Spirit-filled confidence and strength.

As a result of that choice, what truly delights and reveals sons and daughters of God will be evident in our lives. Worship will be genuine, service a joy, humility natural, friendship sincere, giving heartfelt, and caring authentic.

"Grace livers" know that, having already been made a perfect fit for the filling and activity of the Holy Spirit, offering themselves to Him is the primary step toward finding His grace sufficient for all of life. Those who offer themselves will find perfect love and the grace of God. Toward what end? They'll know what kind of service and to whom, how much money to give and where, what to say or not say, what to do or not do, what to like or not like, and more. For you and me it's the way of life, and it keeps heaven in view.

Because many have lost the view of heaven, they've lost the love and joy and grace and motivation which come from it. Though I believe they are secure for eternity, Christ is of no value, no current effect to them—they're lacking life (see Galatians 5:2). *They're in neutral.* But that doesn't mean they aren't busy revving their engines and honking their horns, even urging others to do the same. It's what they know. If you and I try to get them to quit their anxious foot stomping and horn honking without telling them of the grace of God to them in Christ, we'll just be encouraging them to cease hyper-activity for *no* activity. If we don't introduce them to heaven's view they'll still be lifeless—zombies on parade.

What can you do? Keep your own fire lit and your own thirst quenched. It may sound selfish but pretended heat and postured satisfaction are problems enough in the church without you succumbing as well.

In attempting to light fires and create thirst in others over many years of ministry, disappointment in how people receive the truth has at times led to deep personal disillusionment. I have been led away from the very passion and delight I've found with God, having put something else before it—*other people*. While believing that they are His workmanship, I sometimes fall victim to thinking I might help Him out a bit. In that misguided attempt, I can get awfully cold and thirsty and have little to offer. Think of it this way: the best cup from which to drink is the full one—not the *empty* one.

You will be brought before many challenging and trying situations. But the greatest challenge and the highest goal is to keep knowing Jesus and His view of you and everything else. On the job, in your relationships, in your hopes and dreams, in your failures and in your successes (and there will be plenty of both), knowing Him as your greatest treasure will mean satisfaction for you and hope for others. You've sold off everything and bought the field, having discovered Him as your treasure. Pay attention to it, marveling at it, and the byproduct will be the style of life God intends for you and for His glory. Out of love for God, you'll give the Gospel and forgive those who preach a twisted version. You'll see what heaven sees and passionately desire to relieve believers of their earthborn view.

You'll be living from God's astounding opinion of you, and to God's glory, you'll tell them *they're better off than they think*.

This is my prayer for you:

> I pray that out of his glorious riches he may strengthen you with power through his Spirit in your inner being, so that Christ may dwell in your hearts through faith. And I pray that you, being rooted and established in love, may have power, together with all the saints, to grasp how wide and long and high and deep is the love of Christ, and to know this love that surpasses knowledge—that you may be filled to the measure of all the fullness of God. Now to him who is able to do immeasurably more than all we ask or imagine, according to his power that is at work within us, to him be glory in the church and in Christ Jesus throughout all generations, for ever and ever! Amen. (Ephesians 3:16-21)